Stews, Chilies & Chowders

Jean Paré

www.companyscoming.com
visit our ⚜ website

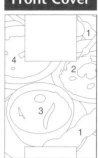

Front Cover

1. Bread Twists, page 138
2. Meatless Wild Rice Chili, page 85
3. Beef Ragoût, page 28
4. Salmon Chowder, page 110

Props Courtesy Of:
Scona Claywork
The Bay

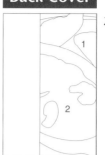

Back Cover

1. Individual Focaccia, page 145
2. Easy Cioppino, page 41

Props Courtesy Of:
The Bay

Stews, Chilies & Chowders

Seventh Printing December 2006

Library and Archives Canada Cataloguing in Publication
Paré, Jean, date
Stews, Chilies & Chowders
(Original series)
Includes index.
ISBN 13: 978-1-895455-63-2
ISBN 10: 1-895455-63-4
1. Stews. 2. Soups. 3. Chili con carne. I. Title.
TX693.P377 2001   641.8'23   C2001-900427-3

Published by
Company's Coming Publishing Limited
2311 – 96 Street
Edmonton, Alberta, Canada T6N 1G3
Tel: 780-450-6223   Fax: 780-450-1857
www.companyscoming.com

Need more recipes?

Six *"sneak preview"* recipes are featured online **with every new book released.**

Visit us at ↘

Company's Coming Cookbooks

Original Series

- Softcover, 160 pages
- 6" x 9" (15 cm x 23 cm) format
- Lay-flat plastic comb binding
- Full-colour photos
- Nutrition information

Quick & easy recipes! Everyday ingredients!

Lifestyle Series

- Softcover, 160 pages
- 8" x 10" (20 cm x 25 cm) format
- Paperback
- Full-colour photos
- Nutrition information

Most Loved Recipe Collection

- Hardcover, 128 pages
- 8 3/4" x 8 3/4" (22 cm x 22 cm) format
- Durable sewn binding
- Full-colour throughout
- Nutrition information

Special Occasion Series

- Hardcover & softcover
- 8 1/2" x 11" (22 cm x 28 cm) format
- Durable sewn binding
- Full-colour throughout
- Nutrition information

See page 157 for more cookbooks.
For a complete listing, visit
www.companyscoming.com

Table of Contents

The Company's Coming Story

Jean Paré (pronounced "jeen PAIR-ee") grew up understanding that the combination of family, friends and home cooking is the best recipe for a good life. From her mother, she learned to appreciate good cooking, while her father praised even her earliest attempts in the kitchen. When Jean left home, she took with her a love of cooking, many family recipes and an intriguing desire to read cookbooks as if they were novels!

"never share a recipe you wouldn't use yourself"

In 1963, when her four children had all reached school age, Jean volunteered to cater the 50th Anniversary of the Vermilion School of Agriculture, now Lakeland College, in Alberta, Canada. Working out of her home, Jean prepared a dinner for more than 1,000 people, which launched a flourishing catering operation that continued for over 18 years. During that time, she had countless opportunities to test new ideas with immediate feedback—resulting in empty plates and contented customers! Whether preparing cocktail sandwiches for a house party or serving a hot meal for 1,500 people, Jean Paré earned a reputation for good food, courteous service and reasonable prices.

As requests for her recipes mounted, Jean was often asked the question, "Why don't you write a cookbook?" Jean responded by teaming up with her son, Grant Lovig, in the fall of 1980 to form Company's Coming Publishing Limited. The publication of *150 Delicious Squares* on April 14, 1981 marked the debut of what would soon become one of the world's most popular cookbook series.

The company has grown since those early days when Jean worked from a spare bedroom in her home. Today, she continues to write recipes while working closely with the staff of the Recipe Factory, as the Company's Coming test kitchen is affectionately known. There she fills the role of mentor, assisting with the development of recipes people most want to use for everyday cooking and easy entertaining. Every Company's Coming recipe is *kitchen-tested* before it's approved for publication.

Jean's daughter, Gail Lovig, is responsible for marketing and distribution, leading a team that includes sales personnel located in major cities across Canada. In addition, Company's Coming cookbooks are published and distributed under licence in the United States, Australia and other world markets. Bestsellers many times over in English, Company's Coming cookbooks have also been published in French and Spanish.

Familiar and trusted in home kitchens around the world, Company's Coming cookbooks are offered in a variety of formats. Highly regarded as kitchen workbooks, the softcover Original Series, with its lay-flat plastic comb binding, is still a favourite among readers.

Jean Paré's approach to cooking has always called for *quick and easy recipes* using *everyday ingredients.* That view has served her well. The recipient of many awards, including the Queen Elizabeth Golden Jubilee medal, Jean was appointed a Member of the Order of Canada, her country's highest lifetime achievement honour.

Jean continues to gain new supporters by adhering to what she calls The Golden Rule of Cooking: *"Never share a recipe you wouldn't use yourself."* It's an approach that works— *millions of times over!*

Foreword

Tossing ingredients in a pot and ending up with something delicious is every busy cook's dream. And a concoction that sends tempting aromas wafting through the house will make the rest of the family hurry to the dinner table. With *Stews, Chilies and Chowders,* there are over 120 hearty recipes to do just that!

The terms "stew" and "chili" can be confusing. A stew usually contains meat, vegetables and a thick broth. To stew is a way of cooking food that is barely covered in liquid and simmering in a pot with a tight-fitting lid for a long period of time. It's great for turning bits of tough meat into tender and succulent morsels, and for blending the flavors of all the ingredients.

Stews, Chilies and Chowders also includes ragoûts and goulashes under the stew heading because of the method of cooking. A ragoût (ra-GOO) is a medley of meat, poultry or fish, with or without vegetables, in a thick, seasoned broth. Goulash (GOO-lahsh) originated in Hungary as a mixture of meat and vegetables flavored with paprika, ranging from mild to hot.

Chili is most often the word applied to hot peppers or the combination of herbs and spices which comprise chili powder: cloves, coriander, cumin, garlic and oregano. We use the term for stews which usually contain beans and chili powder.

Most of the beef stew recipes in this cookbook were tested using inside round, blade or chuck steak. For these stews, any stewing meat can be substituted. Flank or sirloin were tested in recipes that required less

cooking time. Remember that many beans can be substituted in the chili recipes, such as black, black-eyed, or red or white kidney beans.

Under the heading of chowder are thick, rich soups, often containing chunks of fish or vegetables. Also packed into these pages are some terrific go-withs: steaming hot breads and buns, plus pucker-your-mouth pickles and savory preserves that naturally go with each dish. With *Stews, Chilies and Chowders,* a steaming bowl full of delicious flavor is nearby anytime!

Jean Paré

Each recipe has been analyzed using the most up-to-date version of the Canadian Nutrient File from Health Canada, which is based on the United States Department of Agriculture (USDA) Nutrient Data Base. If more than one ingredient is listed (such as "hard margarine or butter"), or a range is given (1 – 2 tsp., 5 – 10 mL) then the first ingredient or amount is used in the analysis. Where an ingredient reads "sprinkle," "optional," or "for garnish," it is not included as part of the nutrition information. Milk, unless stated otherwise, is 1% and cooking oil, unless stated otherwise, is canola.

Margaret Ng, B.Sc. (Hon), M.A.
Registered Dietitian

Chunky Barley Stew

A hearty stew full of delicious vegetables. Feeds a large group.

Medium potatoes, quartered	4	4
Medium carrots, cut lengthwise and crosswise into chunks	4	4
Medium yellow turnips, cut lengthwise and crosswise into chunks	3	3
Medium onions, cut into wedges	3	3
Medium celery ribs, with leaves, cut into chunks	3	3
Boneless inside round (or blade or chuck) steak, trimmed of fat and cubed	2 lbs.	900 g
Cooking oil	1 tbsp.	15 mL
Freshly ground pepper	1/2 tsp.	2 mL
Pearl barley	1/3 cup	75 mL
Water	4 cups	1 L
Can of stewed tomatoes, with juice	14 oz.	398 mL
Beef bouillon powder	2 tbsp.	30 mL
Bay leaf	1	1
Dried thyme, crushed	1/4 tsp.	1 mL
Water	1/2 cup	125 mL
All-purpose flour	3 tbsp.	50 mL

Combine first 5 ingredients in large roaster.

Sear beef in cooking oil in large frying pan until browned on all sides. Add to vegetable mixture.

Add pepper and barley. Stir.

Combine first amount of water, tomatoes with juice, bouillon powder, bay leaf and thyme in large saucepan. Bring to a boil. Pour over beef mixture. Cover. Bake in 325°F (160°C) oven for 2 to 3 hours until beef is tender. Remove and discard bay leaf. Use slotted spoon to remove vegetables and beef to serving bowl. Keep warm. Pour remaining liquid into medium saucepan. There should be about 1 1/2 cups (375 mL).

(continued on next page)

Stir second amount of water into flour in small bowl until smooth. Gradually stir into liquid in saucepan. Heat and stir on medium until boiling and thickened. Pour over beef and vegetables. Makes 15 cups (3.74 L).

1 cup (250 mL): 166 Calories; 2.6 g Total Fat; 363 mg Sodium; 16 g Protein; 20 g Carbohydrate; 3 g Dietary Fiber

---

Porcupine Meatball Stew

An old recipe that always satisfies. This has a long cooking time but only takes 30 minutes to prepare.

Extra lean ground beef	1 lb.	454 g
Finely chopped onion	1/4 cup	60 mL
Garlic clove, minced (or 1/4 tsp., 1 mL, powder)	1	1
Large egg	1	1
Fine dry bread crumbs	1/3 cup	75 mL
Seasoned salt	1 tsp.	5 mL
Pepper	1/8 tsp.	0.5 mL
Long grain white rice, uncooked	1/4 cup	60 mL
Small onion, cut into wedges	1	1
Sliced carrot	2 1/4 cups	550 mL
Medium potatoes, cut into chunks	2	2
Diced green pepper	1/2 cup	125 mL
Can of stewed tomatoes, with juice	14 oz.	398 mL
Water	1/2 cup	125 mL
Beef bouillon powder	1 tsp.	5 mL

Combine first 8 ingredients in medium bowl. Divide and shape into 12 meatballs. Arrange in single layer in bottom of ungreased 2 quart (2 L) casserole.

Layer next 4 ingredients, in order given, over meatballs.

Heat tomatoes with juice, water and bouillon powder in small saucepan until boiling. Pour over vegetables. Cover. Bake in 325°F (160°C) oven for 2 hours. Makes 6 cups (1.5 L).

1 cup (250 mL): 260 Calories; 7.8 g Total Fat; 590 mg Sodium; 18 g Protein; 29 g Carbohydrate; 3 g Dietary Fiber

Mashed Potato-Topped Stew

Garlic mashed potatoes are delicious as a topping for this oven stew.
For less garlic flavor, simply reduce the number of cloves used.

Boneless inside round (or blade or chuck) steak, trimmed of fat and cubed	1 1/2 lbs.	680 g
Sliced carrot	2 cups	500 mL
Medium onion, cut into wedges	1	1
Frozen french-cut green beans	1 1/2 cups	375 mL
Can of stewed tomatoes, with juice	14 oz.	398 mL
Water	1/2 cup	125 mL
Worcestershire sauce	2 tsp.	10 mL
All-purpose flour	1/2 cup	125 mL
Beef bouillon powder	1 tsp.	5 mL
Dry mustard	1 tsp.	5 mL
Dried marjoram	1 tsp.	5 mL
Garlic salt	1 tsp.	5 mL
Medium potatoes, cut into chunks	5	5
Garlic cloves, peeled (to your taste)	5	5
Salt	1 tsp.	5 mL
Water		
Skim milk powder	1/3 cup	75 mL
Hard margarine (or butter)	2 tbsp.	30 mL
Large egg	1	1

Place beef, carrot, onion and beans in ungreased 3 quart (3 L) casserole.

Process next 8 ingredients in blender until smooth. Pour over beef mixture. Stir. Cover. Bake in 325°F (160°C) oven for about 2 hours until beef is tender.

Boil potatoes, garlic and salt in water in medium saucepan for 15 minutes until tender. Drain, leaving about 1/2 cup (125 mL) liquid in saucepan with potatoes.

Add skim milk powder and margarine. Mash until smooth. Add egg. Mash until combined. Spoon potato mixture over beef mixture. Gently smooth surface. Bake, uncovered, for about 20 minutes until potatoes are starting to set and are lightly golden. Makes 14 cups (3.5 L).

1 cup (250 mL): 131 Calories; 3.3 g Total Fat; 288 mg Sodium; 14 g Protein; 11 g Carbohydrate; 1 g Dietary Fiber

Syrian Beef Stew

Mint and cinnamon flavors are evident in this Middle-Eastern stew.

Boneless inside round (or blade or chuck) steak, trimmed of fat and cubed	1 lb.	454 g
Cooking oil	1 tbsp.	15 mL
Chopped onion	1 1/2 cups	375 mL
Garlic clove, minced (or 1/4 tsp., 1 mL, powder)	1	1
Medium roma (plum) tomatoes, seeded and diced	4	4
Can of stewed tomatoes, with juice	14 oz.	398 mL
Lime juice	2 tbsp.	30 mL
Ground cinnamon	1/4 tsp.	1 mL
Turmeric	1/4 tsp.	1 mL
Granulated sugar	1/2 - 3/4 tsp.	2 - 4 mL
Salt	1/2 tsp.	2 mL
Pepper	1/4 tsp.	1 mL
Cut fresh green beans (or frozen, thawed)	3 cups	750 mL
Chopped fresh mint leaves	2 tbsp.	30 mL
Water	1/4 cup	60 mL
Cornstarch	2 tbsp.	30 mL

Sear beef in cooking oil in large frying pan until browned on all sides. Remove with slotted spoon to ungreased 2 quart (2 L) casserole.

Sauté onion and garlic in same frying pan until onion is soft and golden. Add to beef mixture.

Add roma tomatoes, stewed tomatoes with juice, lime juice, cinnamon, turmeric, sugar, salt and pepper. Stir. Cover. Bake in 275°F (140°C) oven for 1 1/2 to 2 hours until beef is tender.

Add green beans and mint. Stir.

Stir water into cornstarch in small cup until smooth. Gradually stir into beef mixture. Cover. Bake for 30 minutes until beans are tender-crisp and sauce is thickened. Makes 6 1/2 cups (1.6 L).

1 cup (250 mL): 198 Calories; 4.5 g Total Fat; 434 mg Sodium; 8 g Protein; 21 g Carbohydrate; 3 g Dietary Fiber

Prairie Roots Pie

Root vegetables and tender beef in a richly-flavored sauce
all under a flaky pastry crust.

All-purpose flour	1 1/2 tbsp.	25 mL
Garlic salt	1/2 tsp.	2 mL
Pepper	1/4 tsp.	1 mL
Boneless inside round (or blade or chuck) steak, trimmed of fat and cubed	3/4 lb.	340 g
Cooking oil	1 1/2 tsp.	7 mL
Medium onion, sliced	1	1
Water	3/4 cup	175 mL
Beef bouillon powder	1/2 tbsp.	7 mL
Large parsnips, peeled, halved and sliced	3	3
Large carrots, peeled and diced	3	3
Potatoes, peeled and diced	1/2 lb.	225 g
Small yellow turnip, peeled and diced	1	1
Parsley flakes	1 tsp.	5 mL
Dried thyme	1/4 tsp.	1 mL
Dried sweet basil	1/4 tsp.	1 mL
Salt	1/4 tsp.	1 mL
Bay leaf	1	1
Water	2 1/2 tbsp.	37 mL
All-purpose flour	1 1/2 tbsp.	25 mL
Pastry, for 2 crust 9 inch (22 cm) pie, your own or a mix		
Parsley flakes	1/4 cup	60 mL

Combine first amount of flour, garlic salt and pepper in medium bowl or resealable plastic bag. Dredge beef in flour mixture until well coated.

Sear beef in cooking oil in medium frying pan until browned on all sides. Remove beef with slotted spoon to greased 3 quart (3 L) casserole.

(continued on next page)

Sauté onion in same frying pan until soft, adding 1 tbsp. (15 mL) water at a time, if necessary, to scrape any brown bits from pan. Add remaining first amount of water and bouillon powder. Stir. Pour over beef.

Add next 9 ingredients to beef mixture. Stir. Cover. Simmer for 2 hours, stirring occasionally, until vegetables are tender.

Stir second amount of water into second amount of flour in small cup until smooth. Gradually stir into stew. Cover. Cook for 15 minutes until thickened. Makes 5 1/2 cups (1.4 L) filling. Cool slightly.

Prepare pastry, adding parsley to dry ingredients. Roll out 1/2 of pastry on lightly floured surface to 1/8 inch (3 mm) thick. Line 9 inch (22 cm) pie plate. Add beef mixture. Roll out second 1/2 of pastry. Cut into 1 inch (2.5 cm) strips. Arrange on top of beef mixture, lattice-style. Seal edges. Bake in 400°F (205°C) oven for 25 to 30 minutes until stew is bubbly and crust is golden. Serves 6.

1 serving: 407 Calories; 16.7 g Total Fat; 682 mg Sodium; 18 g Protein; 47 g Carbohydrate; 4 g Dietary Fiber

Pictured on page 18.

Paré Pointer

The Big Dipper is how milk is put into the Milky Way.

Greek Stew

Spices and currants in this stew make a fragrant aroma in the kitchen.
Serve over rice pilaf or couscous.

Boneless inside round (or blade or chuck) steak, trimmed of fat and cubed	1 lb.	454 g
Olive oil (or cooking oil)	1 tbsp.	15 mL
Coarsely chopped onion	3 cups	750 mL
Olive oil (or cooking oil)	1 tbsp.	15 mL
Garlic cloves, minced (or 1 1/4 tsp., 5 mL, powder), or less if desired	5	5
Ground cinnamon	1 1/2 tsp.	7 mL
Ground cloves	1/2 tsp.	2 mL
Cans of diced tomatoes (14 oz., 398 mL, each), with juice	2	2
Dry red (or alcohol-free) wine	2 cups	500 mL
Currants	2/3 cup	150 mL
Water	1/3 cup	75 mL
Cornstarch	3 tbsp.	50 mL

Chopped roma (plum) tomatoes,
    for garnish
Sliced kalamata olives, for garnish

Sear beef in first amount of olive oil in large pot or Dutch oven until browned on all sides. Remove beef with slotted spoon to medium bowl.

Sauté onion in same pot in second amount of olive oil, stirring frequently, until soft and golden.

Add garlic. Stir. Sprinkle with cinnamon and cloves. Stir. Sauté until well combined and mixture is fragrant.

Add tomatoes with juice, wine and currants. Stir. Bring to a boil. Add beef. Stir. Cover. Simmer for about 2 hours until beef is tender.

(continued on next page)

Stir water into cornstarch in small cup until smooth. Gradually stir into stew. Heat and stir for about 5 minutes until thickened.

Sprinkle tomato and olives on individual servings. Makes 9 cups (2.25 L).

1 cup (250 mL): 192 Calories; 4.6 g Total Fat; 184 mg Sodium; 15 g Protein; 14 g Carbohydrate; 2 g Dietary Fiber

Variation: Add 10 oz. (300 g) package frozen chopped spinach, thawed and squeezed dry, and 1 tbsp. (15 mL) brown sugar 15 minutes before end of cooking time.

Easy-Does-It Oven Stew

Tapioca thickens the gravy in this one-step stew.
Serve over noodles or with mashed potatoes.

Boneless inside round (or blade or chuck) steak, trimmed of fat and cubed	1 1/2 lbs.	680 g
Sliced carrot	1 1/2 cups	375 mL
Sliced celery	1 1/4 cups	300 mL
Fresh medium mushrooms, quartered	8	8
Green onions, sliced	4	4
Can of stewed tomatoes, with juice	14 oz.	398 mL
Water	1 cup	250 mL
Dry red (or alcohol-free) wine	1/2 cup	125 mL
Minute tapioca	3 tbsp.	50 mL
Beef bouillon powder	1 tbsp.	15 mL
Bay leaf	1	1
Italian no-salt seasoning (such as Mrs. Dash)	1 1/2 tsp.	7 mL
Pepper	1/4 tsp.	1 mL

Place all 13 ingredients in ungreased 4 quart (4 L) casserole. Stir. Cover. Bake in 325°F (160°C) oven for about 3 hours until beef is tender. Remove and discard bay leaf. Makes 6 cups (1.5 L).

1 cup (250 mL): 210 Calories; 2.8 g Total Fat; 566 mg Sodium; 28 g Protein; 15 g Carbohydrate; 2 g Dietary Fiber

Squash Stew

Full of autumn colors! Beef is moist and tender and veggies are well cooked but not overdone.

Boneless chuck (or blade or inside round) steak, trimmed of fat and cubed	1 lb.	454 g
Coarsely chopped onion	1 cup	250 mL
Diced potato	3 cups	750 mL
Sliced carrot	3 cups	750 mL
Acorn squash, peeled and cubed	2 lbs.	900 g
Beef bouillon powder	2 tsp.	10 mL
Boiling water	1/2 cup	125 mL
Can of tomato sauce	7 1/2 oz.	213 mL
Granulated sugar	1/2 tsp.	2 mL
Salt	1/2 tsp.	2 mL
Pepper	1/8 tsp.	0.5 mL

Layer beef, onion, potato, carrot and squash in ungreased 4 quart (4 L) casserole or small roaster.

Dissolve bouillon powder in boiling water in medium bowl. Add tomato sauce, sugar, salt and pepper. Stir well. Pour over vegetables. Cover. Bake in 300°F (150°C) oven for 3 1/2 to 4 hours until beef is tender and vegetables are cooked. Makes about 10 cups (2.5 L).

1 cup (250 mL): 149 Calories; 3.6 g Total Fat; 423 mg Sodium; 11 g Protein; 20 g Carbohydrate; 3 g Dietary Fiber

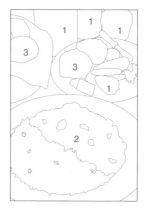

1. Hot Pickled Peppers, page 148
2. Green Chili Stew, page 31
3. Pumpkin Corn Cakes, page 142

Props Courtesy of: Bernardin Ltd.
Stokes

Indonesian Beef

The dark brown sauce is spicy with just a hint of sweetness and there's plenty of it to serve over rice.

Garlic cloves, minced (or 1 tsp., 4 mL, powder)	4	4
Salt	1/2 tsp.	2 mL
Freshly grated gingerroot	2 tsp.	10 mL
Ground cardamom	3/4 tsp.	4 mL
Ground cinnamon	1 tsp.	5 mL
Ground nutmeg	1/2 tsp.	2 mL
Ground cloves	1/8 tsp.	0.5 mL
Brown sugar, packed	2 tbsp.	30 mL
Freshly ground pepper	1/2 tsp.	2 mL
Boneless inside round (or blade or chuck) steak, trimmed of fat and cubed	2 lbs.	900 g
Cooking oil	1 tbsp.	15 mL
Finely chopped onion	2 cups	500 mL
Hot water	1 cup	250 mL
Soy sauce	1/3 cup	75 mL

Combine first 8 ingredients in small bowl. Stir until paste-like consistency. Set aside.

Sprinkle pepper over beef. Sear beef in cooking oil in large frying pan until starting to brown. Add onion. Stir. Cook for about 5 minutes until onion is soft and clear. Add reserved spice mixture. Stir. Heat and stir for about 5 minutes until onion is soft and golden.

Add hot water and soy sauce. Stir. Cover. Simmer on low for 1 to 1 1/2 hours until beef is tender. Stir. Cook, uncovered, until beef is tender and sauce is reduced and thickened slightly. Makes 4 1/2 cups (1.1 L).

1 cup (250 mL): 336 Calories; 7.6 g Total Fat; 1666 mg Sodium; 50 g Protein; 16 g Carbohydrate; 1 g Dietary Fiber

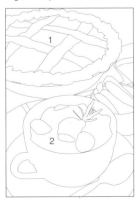

1. Prairie Roots Pie, page 12
2. Bourguignonne Stew, page 22

Props Courtesy Of: Winners Stores

Stews

Bœuf En Daube Canadien

This stew's wonderful aroma is sealed in under the crust,
ready to burst forth with the first serving.

Bacon slices, diced	5	5
All-purpose flour	3 tbsp.	50 mL
Seasoned salt	1/2 tsp.	2 mL
Pepper	1/2 tsp.	2 mL
Garlic powder	1/2 tsp.	2 mL
Boneless inside round (or blade or chuck) steak, trimmed of fat and cubed	2 1/2 lbs.	1.1 kg
Whole small fresh mushrooms	2 cups	500 mL
Small onions, quartered	3	3
Brandy	1/4 cup	60 mL
Dry red (or alcohol-free) wine	1 cup	250 mL
Baby carrots	1/2 lb.	225 g
All-purpose flour	1/4 cup	60 mL
Beef bouillon powder	4 tsp.	20 mL
Parsley flakes	2 tsp.	10 mL
Dried marjoram	1/4 tsp.	1 mL
Dried thyme	1/4 tsp.	1 mL
Bay leaves	2	2
Salt	1/4 tsp.	1 mL
Pepper	1/2 tsp.	2 mL
Ground cloves, sprinkle		
Water	1 1/4 cups	300 mL
Pastry, for 2 crust 9 inch (22 cm) pie, your own or a mix	1	1
Milk	1 tbsp.	15 mL

Fry bacon in large frying pan until crisp. Remove with slotted spoon to ungreased 4 quart (4 L) casserole. Reserve 2 tbsp. (30 mL) drippings in frying pan.

(continued on next page)

Combine flour, seasoned salt, pepper and garlic powder in medium bowl or resealable plastic bag. Dredge beef in flour mixture until well coated. Sear beef in reserved drippings, in 2 batches, until browned on all sides. Remove with slotted spoon to casserole.

Sauté mushrooms and onion in same frying pan until starting to brown. Add to beef mixture. Stir.

Add brandy to same frying pan. Heat and stir, scraping any brown bits from sides and bottom of pan. Pour over beef mixture. Add red wine and carrots to beef mixture. Stir well.

Measure next 9 ingredients into small saucepan. Stir in water. Heat and stir until boiling and slightly thickened. Pour over beef mixture. Stir gently. Lightly pack down surface to make level. Makes 9 cups (2.25 L).

Prepare pastry. Roll out 2/3 of dough to 1 1/2 inches (3.8 cm) larger than casserole surface. Place over casserole. Fold excess pastry under edge. Flute edge against casserole dish to seal tightly. Roll out remaining pie dough to 1/8 inch (3 mm) thickness. Cut out desired shapes. Brush shapes with milk. Lay in attractive design over crust. Bake in 300°F (150°C) oven for about 2 1/2 hours until crust is nicely browned. Serves 8.

1 serving: 401 Calories; 14 g Total Fat; 706 mg Sodium; 37 g Protein; 21 g Carbohydrate; 1 g Dietary Fiber

 When making pastry, measure ingredients accurately. Pastry can be tough with too much flour. Too much shortening results in greasy or crumbly pastry. As well, too much handling can make a pastry tough.

Bourguignonne Stew

A rich-flavored beef and wine stew that can be served as is or over broad noodles. Elegant enough for company.

Water		
Rosemary sprig (or 1 tsp., 5 mL, dried)	1	1
Unpeeled baby red potatoes, cut in half	1 lb.	454 g
Whole baby carrots	1/2 lb.	225 g
Freshly ground pepper, generous sprinkle		
Boneless rib-eye steaks, trimmed of fat and cubed	1 lb.	454 g
Cooking oil	2 tsp.	10 mL
Small onion, cut into wedges	1	1
Garlic clove, minced (or 1/4 tsp., 1 mL, powder)	1	1
Sliced fresh mushrooms	2 cups	500 mL
Can of condensed beef broth	10 oz.	284 mL
Bay leaves	2	2
Dry red (or alcohol-free) wine	1/2 cup	125 mL
All-purpose flour	1 1/2 tsp.	7 mL
Cornstarch	1 1/2 tsp.	7 mL

Bring water and rosemary to a boil under steamer basket or insert. Place potato and carrot in basket. Cover. Steam for 15 minutes until tender-crisp. Place vegetables in large bowl. Keep warm.

Sprinkle pepper over beef. Sear in cooking oil in large frying pan until browned on all sides. Remove beef with slotted spoon to vegetable mixture. Keep warm.

Sauté onion and garlic in same frying pan, stirring frequently, until onion is soft. Add mushrooms. Sauté until mushrooms are golden and liquid is absorbed. Add broth and bay leaves. Stir. Boil, uncovered, for 5 to 10 minutes until liquid is slightly reduced.

Stir wine into flour and cornstarch in small cup until smooth. Gradually stir into mushroom mixture. Heat and stir until boiling and thickened. Remove and discard bay leaves. Pour gravy over beef mixture. Stir gently to combine and heat through. Makes 7 cups (1.75 L).

1 cup (250 mL): 210 Calories; 6.1 g Total Fat; 338 mg Sodium; 18 g Protein; 18 g Carbohydrate; 3 g Dietary Fiber

Pictured on page 18.

Quick Beef Pot Pie

*Old-fashioned taste using convenience foods from the cupboard
and leftover roast beef.*

Can of ready-to-serve chunky beef and barley soup	19 oz.	540 mL
Diced cooked roast beef	2 cups	500 mL
Frozen mixed peas and carrots, thawed and drained	3/4 cup	175 mL
Frozen kernel corn, thawed and drained	1/2 cup	125 mL
Seasoned salt	1/4 tsp.	1 mL
Garlic powder	1/8 tsp.	0.5 mL
Pepper	1/8 tsp.	0.5 mL
Grated medium Cheddar cheese	1/2 cup	125 mL
Can of french-fried onions	2 3/4 oz.	79 g
Refrigerator buttermilk biscuits (10 biscuits per tube)	12 oz.	340 g
Grated medium Cheddar cheese	1/2 cup	125 mL

Heat soup in large saucepan until hot.

Add next 6 ingredients. Stir. Heat until just boiling.

Add first amount of cheese and 1/2 of onions. Stir. Pour into greased
2 quart (2 L) casserole.

Cut biscuits in half crosswise. Arrange, cut side down, on top of stew, all
around edge of casserole. Any extra biscuit pieces can be pressed together
and placed in center of stew. Bake in 350°F (175°C) oven for 25 to
30 minutes until biscuits are golden. Sprinkle with second amount of
cheese and remaining 1/2 of onions. Bake for 5 minutes until cheese is
melted. Makes 4 cups (1 L) stew.

*1 cup (250 mL): 713 Calories; 32 g Total Fat; 1870 mg Sodium; 43 g Protein; 64 g Carbohydrate;
2 g Dietary Fiber*

Short-Rib Borscht Stew

Rich red beet sauce surrounding hearty amounts of ribs and vegetables.
Makes a large batch.

Boneless beef short-ribs, trimmed of fat	3 lbs.	1.4 kg
Cooking oil	1 tbsp.	15 mL
Sliced carrot	2 cups	500 mL
Large onion, sliced	1	1
Julienned yellow turnip, (see Tip, page 25)	1 1/2 cups	375 mL
Sliced celery	1 cup	250 mL
Diced parsnip	3/4 cup	175 mL
Water	2 3/4 cups	675 mL
Can of condensed beef broth	10 oz.	284 mL
Can of tomato paste	5 1/2 oz.	156 mL
Seasoned salt	1 tsp.	5 mL
Pepper	1/4 tsp.	1 mL
Medium beets, peeled and cut julienne (see Tip, page 25)	4	4
Small head of cabbage (about 2 lbs., 900 g), coarsely chopped	1	1
Hot water	1 cup	250 mL
Granulated sugar	1 tbsp.	15 mL
White vinegar	1 tbsp.	15 mL

Sour cream, for garnish

Sear short-ribs in cooking oil in large frying pan until browned on all sides. Drain. Blot with paper towel. Place in ungreased large roaster.

Add carrot, onion, turnip, celery and parsnip. Stir.

Combine first amount of water, broth and tomato paste in small bowl. Pour over beef mixture. Sprinkle with seasoned salt and pepper. Stir. Cover. Bake in 350° (175°C) oven for about 2 hours until ribs are tender.

Add beets. Stir.

(continued on next page)

Layer cabbage over beef mixture.

Stir second amount of water, sugar and vinegar in small bowl until sugar is dissolved. Pour over cabbage. Do not stir. Cover. Cook for 2 hours until beef and beets are tender.

Garnish individual servings with dollop of sour cream. Makes 16 cups (4 L).

1 cup (250 mL): 434 Calories; 20 g Total Fat; 615 mg Sodium; 39 g Protein; 25 g Carbohydrate; 6 g Dietary Fiber

LIGHT BORSCHT STEW: Omit short-ribs. Add 1 1/2 lbs. (680 g) lean beef stewing meat.

 To cut vegetables julienne, cut into 1/8 inch (3 mm) strips that resemble matchsticks.

Paré Pointer

What a shame the astronauts couldn't land on the moon. It was full.

Stews

Chinese Stew

Noodles, vegetables and beef in one dish.
Ginger and chili paste make the sauce spicy hot.

Sirloin steak, cut diagonally into thin strips	1 lb.	454 g
Prepared orange juice	1 cup	250 mL
Water	1 cup	250 mL
Soy sauce	2 tbsp.	30 mL
Sherry (or alcohol-free sherry)	1 tbsp.	15 mL
Beef bouillon powder	2 tsp.	10 mL
Brown sugar, packed	2 tsp.	10 mL
Ground ginger	1 tsp.	5 mL
Hot chili paste (see Note)	1 tsp.	5 mL
Garlic cloves, minced (or 1/2 tsp., 2 mL, powder)	2	2
Cellophane (bean thread) noodles (see Note)	4 oz.	114 g
Boiling water	6 cups	1.5 L
Coarsely shredded Chinese cabbage	3 cups	750 mL
Medium red pepper, slivered	1	1
Medium onion, cut into 12 wedges	1	1
Water	2 tbsp.	30 mL
Cornstarch	4 tsp.	20 mL

Place first 10 ingredients in large pot or Dutch oven. Bring to a boil, stirring constantly. Reduce heat. Cover. Simmer for 30 minutes until beef is tender.

Cover noodles with boiling water in large bowl. Let stand for 2 minutes. Drain.

Add cabbage, red pepper and onion to beef mixture. Stir. Cover. Simmer for 8 to 10 minutes until vegetables are tender-crisp. Add noodles. Stir. Cover. Cook for 2 to 3 minutes.

Stir water into cornstarch in small cup until smooth. Gradually stir into stew. Heat and stir until boiling and thickened. Makes 7 cups (1.75 L).

1 cup (250 mL): 197 Calories; 2.9 g Total Fat; 814 mg Sodium; 18 g Protein; 24 g Carbohydrate; 2 g Dietary Fiber

Note: Available in Asian section of grocery store.

Shredded Beef And Peppers

Thick with meat and peppers. The jalapeños add a nice nip.
Serve with rice or mashed potatoes.

Water	1 1/2 cups	375 mL
Beef bouillon powder	2 tsp.	10 mL
Spicy barbecue sauce	1/2 cup	125 mL
Chopped onion	1 cup	250 mL
Diced carrot	2 cups	500 mL
Bay leaf	1	1
Beef flank steak, trimmed of fat and cut into 3 pieces	1 1/2 lbs.	680 g
Green pepper, sliced	1	1
Red pepper, sliced	1	1
Yellow pepper, sliced	1	1
Can of stewed tomatoes, with liquid	14 oz.	398 mL
Jalapeño peppers, seeded and diced (see Note)	2 - 3	2 - 3
Potato flakes	1/2 cup	125 mL

Place first 7 ingredients in order given in ungreased 4 quart (4 L) casserole or medium roaster. Cover. Bake in 300°F (150°C) oven for about 2 1/2 hours until beef is tender. Remove lid. Remove beef. Shred beef with 2 forks into long strands. Remove and discard bay leaf. Return beef to casserole.

Add remaining 6 ingredients. Stir. Cover. Bake for about 30 minutes until peppers are tender-crisp. Makes 10 cups (2.5 L).

1 cup (250 mL): 174 Calories; 5.6 g Total Fat; 398 mg Sodium; 17 g Protein; 14 g Carbohydrate; 3 g Dietary Fiber

Note: Wear gloves when chopping jalapeño peppers and avoid touching your eyes.

Beef Ragoût

Hearty beef flavor is sweetened with caramelized onions.
Serve this colorful, chunky stew over mashed potatoes.

Chopped onion	2 cups	500 mL
Garlic cloves, minced (or 1/2 tsp., 2 mL, powder)	2	2
Hard margarine (or butter)	2 tbsp.	30 mL
Boneless inside round (or blade or chuck) steak, trimmed of fat and cubed	2 lbs.	900 g
Reserved tomato juice, plus water to make	1 cup	250 mL
Bay leaves	2	2
Pepper	1/4 tsp.	1 mL
Whole baby carrots	2 cups	500 mL
Whole small fresh mushrooms	2 cups	500 mL
Can of stewed tomatoes, drained and juice reserved	14 oz.	398 mL
Medium green pepper, slivered	1	1
Paprika	2 tsp.	10 mL
Seasoned salt	1 tsp.	5 mL
Water	1/3 cup	75 mL
All-purpose flour	2 tbsp.	30 mL

Sauté onion and garlic in margarine in large frying pan until onion is soft and golden. Turn into ungreased 3 quart (3 L) casserole.

Add beef. Add tomato juice mixture, bay leaves and pepper. Stir. Cover. Bake in 325°F (160°C) oven for 1 1/2 hours.

Add next 6 ingredients. Stir. Cover. Bake for about 1 hour until beef is very tender. Remove and discard bay leaves.

Stir water into flour in small cup until smooth. Gradually stir into beef mixture. Cover. Bake for 15 minutes until bubbling and thickened. Makes 10 cups (2.5 L).

(continued on next page)

Pictured on front cover.

Slow Cooker Method: Sauté onion and garlic in margarine in frying pan until onion is soft and golden. Place in 4 quart (4 L) slow cooker. Add next 10 ingredients. Cover. Cook on Low for 8 to 10 hours or on High for 4 to 5 hours. Remove and discard bay leaves. Stir water into flour in small cup until smooth. Stir into beef mixture. Cover. Cook for 15 minutes on High until bubbling and thickened.

Stand-By Beef Stew

No pre-browning necessary. The cans of soup make the gravy.
Serve over mashed potatoes or rice.

Boneless inside round (or blade or chuck) steak, trimmed of fat and cubed	3 lbs.	1.4 kg
Medium carrots, cut into chunks	6	6
Medium onions, cut into wedges	2	2
Garlic cloves, minced (or 1/2 tsp., 2 mL, powder), optional	2	2
Can of condensed cream of mushroom soup	10 oz.	284 mL
Can of condensed cream of tomato soup	10 oz.	284 mL
Sherry (or alcohol-free sherry), or water	1/2 cup	125 mL

Place first 4 ingredients in ungreased medium roaster or 4 quart (4 L) casserole.

Combine both soups and sherry in small bowl. Pour over beef mixture. Stir gently. Cover. Bake in 325°F (160°C) oven for 3 1/2 to 4 hours until beef is very tender. Makes 8 1/2 cups (2.1 L).

Slow Cooker Method: Assemble all 7 ingredients in 4 1/2 quart (4.5 L) slow cooker. Cook on low for 7 to 8 hours.

Stroganoff Stew

All the good flavor of a rich creamy stroganoff.

All-purpose flour	2 tbsp.	30 mL
Pepper	1/4 tsp.	1 mL
Boneless inside round (or blade or chuck) steak, trimmed of fat and sliced into 1/4 inch (6 mm) strips	1 lb.	454 g
Cooking oil	1 tbsp.	15 mL
Sliced fresh mushrooms	3 cups	750 mL
Chopped onion	1 cup	250 mL
Garlic cloves, minced (or 1/2 tsp., 2 mL, powder)	2	2
Salt	1/2 tsp.	2 mL
Seasoned salt	1/4 tsp.	1 mL
Can of condensed beef broth	10 oz.	284 mL
Water	1 cup	250 mL
Diced potato	2 cups	500 mL
Sliced carrot	1 1/2 cups	375 mL
Water	1/2 cup	125 mL
All-purpose flour	2 tbsp.	30 mL
Sour cream	1 cup	250 mL

Combine flour and pepper in medium bowl or resealable plastic bag. Dredge beef in flour mixture until well coated. Sear beef in cooking oil in large frying pan until browned on all sides. Remove with slotted spoon to plate.

Sauté next 5 ingredients in same frying pan, stirring frequently, until mushrooms are starting to brown and liquid is evaporated.

Add beef, beef broth and water. Cover. Simmer for 40 minutes.

Add potato and carrot. Stir. Cover. Simmer for 45 minutes until potato is tender. Remove most of beef and vegetables with slotted spoon to serving dish. Keep warm.

Stir water into flour in small cup until smooth. Add sour cream. Stir until smooth. Gradually stir into broth in frying pan. Heat and stir until boiling and thickened. Pour over beef mixture. Stir gently until combined. Makes 10 cups (2.5 L).

1 cup (250 mL): 274 Calories; 10.2 g Total Fat; 648 mg Sodium; 23 g Protein; 23 g Carbohydrate; 3 g Dietary Fiber

Green Chili Stew

Serve this colorful stew with orzo pasta or rice. Deep brown sauce with a peppery bite from the chilies.

Baby carrots, cut into thirds	1/2 lb.	225 g
Finely chopped onion	1 cup	250 mL
Can of diced green chilies, with liquid	4 oz.	114 mL
Medium red pepper, diced	1	1
Garlic cloves, minced (or 1/2 tsp., 2 mL, powder)	2	2
All-purpose flour	3 tbsp.	50 mL
Chili powder	1 tbsp.	15 mL
Dried whole oregano	1 tsp.	5 mL
Ground cumin	1/2 tsp.	2 mL
Boneless inside round (or blade or chuck) steak, trimmed of fat and cubed	2 lbs.	900 g
Cooking oil	1 tbsp.	15 mL
Water	1/2 cup	125 mL
All-purpose flour	1 tbsp.	15 mL
Dry red (or alcohol-free) wine	1/2 cup	125 mL
Beef bouillon powder	1 - 1 1/2 tsp.	5 - 7 mL

Chopped fresh parsley, for garnish

Combine first 5 ingredients in ungreased 3 quart (3 L) casserole.

Combine first amount of flour, chili powder, oregano and cumin in medium bowl or resealable plastic bag. Dredge 1/2 of beef in flour mixture until well coated. Sear beef in cooking oil in large frying pan until browned on all sides. Remove beef with slotted spoon to onion mixture. Stir. Repeat with remaining 1/2 of beef.

Stir water into second amount of flour in small bowl until smooth. Stir in wine. Heat and stir on medium in same frying pan until brown bits are loosened and liquid is thickened.

Add bouillon powder. Stir. Pour over stew. Stir gently. Cover. Bake in 325°F (160°C) oven for about 2 1/2 hours until beef is very tender.

Garnish with parsley. Makes 6 cups (1.5 L).

1 cup (250 mL): 270 Calories; 6 g Total Fat; 336 mg Sodium; 37 g Protein; 13 g Carbohydrate; 2 g Dietary Fiber

Pictured on page 17.

Stews

Chicken And Dumplings

In France it's called "fricassée". We put dumplings on it and call it stew.
It's every bit as good! The secret to the flavor is the broth.

Chicken parts, skin removed	3 1/2 lbs.	1.6 kg
Water	5 cups	1.25 L
Medium carrot, cut into 4 pieces	1	1
Coarsely chopped celery, with leaves	1 1/2 cups	375 mL
Small onion, quartered	1	1
Bay leaf	1	1
Whole black peppercorns	2 tsp.	10 mL
Salt	2 tsp.	10 mL
Chopped onion	1 1/2 cups	375 mL
Sliced celery	1 cup	250 mL
Hard margarine (or butter)	2 tbsp.	30 mL
Diced carrot	2 cups	500 mL
Parsley flakes	1 tbsp.	15 mL
Pepper	1/4 tsp.	1 mL
Frozen peas, thawed	1 cup	250 mL
Skim evaporated milk	2/3 cup	150 mL
All-purpose flour	1/3 cup	75 mL
TOMATO DUMPLINGS		
All-purpose flour	2 cups	500 mL
Baking powder	3 tsp.	15 mL
Salt	1/2 tsp.	2 mL
Parsley flakes	1 tsp.	5 mL
Onion powder	1/4 tsp.	1 mL
Large egg	1	1
Cooking oil	1 tbsp.	15 mL
Tomato juice	3/4 cup	175 mL
Sliced green onion	1/3 cup	75 mL

(continued on next page)

Combine chicken and water in large pot or Dutch oven. Bring to a boil. Skim off any grey foam as it forms.

Add next 6 ingredients. Cover. Simmer on medium-low for 1 hour. Remove chicken with slotted spoon. Cool enough to handle. Remove chicken from bones. Cut chicken into chunks. Set aside. Strain broth, discarding solids. Measure 3 cups (750 mL) broth. Set aside.

Sauté second amounts of onion and celery in margarine in large saucepan until soft.

Add second amount of carrot, reserved broth, parsley flakes and pepper. Stir. Bring to a boil. Reduce heat. Simmer, uncovered, for 20 minutes.

Add peas. Stir.

Stir evaporated milk into flour in small bowl until smooth. Stir into carrot mixture. Heat and stir until boiling and thickened. Turn into greased 3 quart (3 L) casserole. Add chicken. Stir. Makes 8 cups (2 L).

Tomato Dumplings: Combine first 5 ingredients in medium bowl.

Beat egg and cooking oil in small bowl. Beat in tomato juice. Add, all at once, to flour mixture. Add green onion. Stir until moist dough is formed. Drop by large spoonfuls in single layer over top of stew. Bake, uncovered, in 425°F (220°C) oven for 20 minutes until bubbling and dumplings are firm and browned. Serves 8.

1 serving: 370 Calories; 8.7 g Total Fat; 1170 mg Sodium; 29 g Protein; 43 g Carbohydrate; 4 g Dietary Fiber

Pictured on page 36.

 Leftover beef or chicken broth can be frozen for later use in soups or other stews.

All-In-A-Pot Chicken Stew

Thicken the base, throw everything into one pot, and relax for 30 minutes!

Can of condensed chicken broth	10 oz.	284 mL
Water	1/3 cup	75 mL
All-purpose flour	1/4 cup	60 mL
Boneless, skinless chicken breast halves (about 4), cubed	1 lb.	454 g
Broccoli florets (halved if large)	3 cups	750 mL
Baby red potatoes, quartered	8	8
Green onions, cut into 1/2 inch (12 mm) pieces	4	4
Chopped fresh parsley (or 1 tsp., 5 mL, flakes)	4 tsp.	20 mL

Place broth, water and flour in glass jar with tight-fitting lid. Shake vigorously until smooth. Pour into large saucepan. Heat and stir until boiling and thickened.

Stir in remaining 5 ingredients. Heat and stir until just starting to simmer. Cover. Cook on medium-low for 30 minutes until potatoes are tender and chicken is no longer pink. Makes 6 cups (1.5 L).

1 cup (250 mL): 237 Calories; 2.1 g Total Fat; 377 mg Sodium; 24 g Protein; 31 g Carbohydrate; 4 g Dietary Fiber

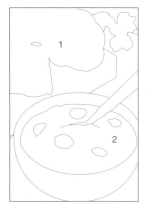

1. Pine Nut Bread Ring, page 130
2. Rich Seafood Stew, page 40

Props Courtesy Of: The Bay

Stewed Chicken
In Sweet Onion Sauce

This stew is served because of its taste, not its looks.
Strong onion and garlic sauce over very tender chicken.

Very thinly sliced onion, separated	10 cups	2.5 L
Garlic cloves, minced (or 1 1/4 tsp., 5 mL, powder)	5	5
Freshly squeezed lemon juice	1/3 cup	75 mL
Grated lemon peel	1 tsp.	5 mL
Cayenne pepper	1/4 tsp.	1 mL
Skinless chicken parts	3 1/2 lbs.	1.6 kg
Cooking oil	2 tbsp.	30 mL
Brown sugar, packed	1 1/2 tbsp.	25 mL

Combine first 6 ingredients in large non-metal bowl or resealable plastic bag. Cover or seal. Marinate in refrigerator for 10 hours or overnight. Remove chicken, reserving marinade. Blot chicken dry with paper towel.

Sear chicken, in 2 batches, in cooking oil in large frying pan on all sides until browned. Place in ungreased 3 quart (3 L) casserole. Add reserved marinade. Cover. Bake in 300°F (150°C) oven for 2 1/2 to 3 hours until chicken is very tender. Remove chicken with slotted spoon to serving platter. Keep warm.

Turn onion mixture into large frying pan. Sprinkle with brown sugar. Bring to a boil. Boil rapidly, uncovered, for about 20 minutes, stirring frequently, until liquid is evaporated and onion is soft and golden. Makes 2 1/4 cups (550 mL) onion sauce. Spoon onion sauce over chicken. Makes about 6 cups (1.5 L).

1 cup (250 mL): 320 Calories; 8.7 g Total Fat; 112 mg Sodium; 31 g Protein; 30 g Carbohydrate; 5 g Dietary Fiber

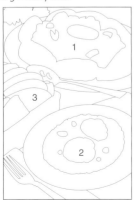

1. Pork And Cabbage Stew, page 50
2. Chicken And Dumplings, page 32
3. Multigrain Bread, page 129

Props Courtesy Of:
    Alberta Craft Council Craft Gallery Shop

African Stew

Peanut butter and coconut milk make a tasty broth in this dark, coral–colored stew. The peanuts are a nice crunchy surprise! A unique stew.

Skinless chicken parts, bone-in	3 lbs.	1.4 kg
Medium onion, cut in half lengthwise and sliced	1	1
Can of condensed chicken broth	10 oz.	284 mL
Water	2/3 cup	150 mL
Can of tomatoes, with juice	14 oz.	398 mL
Coconut milk	1 cup	250 mL
Smooth peanut butter	1/3 cup	75 mL
All-purpose flour	2 tbsp.	30 mL
Dried crushed chilies	1/2 tsp.	2 mL
Chopped red pepper	1 cup	250 mL
Hot cooked long grain white rice (about 1 1/4 cups, 300 mL, uncooked)	4 cups	1 L
Hard-boiled eggs, coarsely chopped	3	3
Chopped roasted peanuts	1/2 cup	125 mL

Place first 4 ingredients in large pot or Dutch oven. Cover. Simmer for 1 hour.

Process tomatoes with juice, coconut milk, peanut butter, flour and chilies in blender until smooth. Add to chicken mixture. Add red pepper. Stir. Cover. Cook for 10 minutes.

Place about 1/2 cup (125 mL) rice into wide individual soup bowls. Divide and sprinkle egg and peanuts over rice. Ladle stew over top. Makes about 8 cups (2 L).

1 cup (250 mL): 489 Calories; 22.2 g Total Fat; 467 mg Sodium; 31 g Protein; 42 g Carbohydrate; 3 g Dietary Fiber

Variation: Add 10 oz. (285 g) shelled and deveined medium shrimp to stew for last 15 minutes of cooking time.

Quick Brunswick Stew

Traditionally made with squirrel meat and cooked slowly for a long period of time, this version has all the flavor but can be on the table in one hour.

Seasoned salt	1 tsp.	5 mL
Pepper	1/4 tsp.	1 mL
Boneless, skinless chicken breast halves (about 2), cut into 1 inch (2.5 cm) cubes	1/2 lb.	225 g
Hard margarine (or butter)	1 tbsp.	15 mL
Can of stewed tomatoes, with juice	14 oz.	398 mL
Can of condensed chicken broth	10 oz.	284 mL
Water	1 cup	250 mL
Chopped onion	1 cup	250 mL
Diced potato	2 cups	500 mL
Can of lima (or butter) beans, drained and rinsed	14 oz.	398 mL
Frozen kernel corn, thawed	1 1/2 cups	375 mL
Sliced fresh okra, cut 1/2 inch (12 mm) thick (or 8 - 10 okra pods)	1 cup	250 mL
Worcestershire sauce	1 tbsp.	15 mL
Granulated sugar	1 tsp.	5 mL
Dried crushed chilies	1/4 tsp.	1 mL

Sprinkle seasoned salt and pepper over chicken. Sear chicken in margarine in large pot or Dutch oven until no longer pink.

Add next 5 ingredients. Stir. Bring to a boil. Cover. Simmer for 15 minutes until potato is tender.

Add remaining 6 ingredients. Stir. Cover. Simmer on medium-low for 25 minutes until thickened. Makes 8 cups (2 L).

1 cup (250 mL): 181 Calories; 2.9 g Total Fat; 652 mg Sodium; 13 g Protein; 26 g Carbohydrate; 5 g Dietary Fiber

Rich Seafood Stew

Richly flavored with the fruits of the sea. Beautiful red base with all the flavors, even the wine, blending nicely. An awesome stew. Also known as cioppino (chup-PEE-noh), an Italian fish stew.

Medium leeks (white and tender parts only), thinly sliced	2	2
Garlic cloves, minced (or 3/4 tsp., 3 mL, powder)	3	3
Chopped green pepper	1/2 cup	125 mL
Olive (or cooking) oil	2 tbsp.	30 mL
Hard margarine (or butter)	1 tbsp.	15 mL
Whole small fresh mushrooms (or medium, halved)	3 cups	750 mL
Can of stewed tomatoes, with juice, mashed	14 oz.	398 mL
Dry red (or alcohol-free) wine	1 1/2 cups	375 mL
Can of tomato paste	5 1/2 oz.	156 mL
Lemon juice	3 tbsp.	50 mL
Dried sweet basil	2 tsp.	10 mL
Dried whole oregano	1/2 tsp.	2 mL
Bay leaf	1	1
Uncooked lobster tail, cut into 1 inch (2.5 cm) pieces	8 oz.	225 g
Uncooked medium shrimp (about 8 oz., 225 g), peeled and deveined	24	24
Fresh (or frozen) small bay scallops (about 10 oz., 285 g)	1 1/2 cups	375 mL
King (or Snow) crab legs, not shelled, broken into pieces (or 9 oz., 255 g, imitation crab chunks)	1 lb.	454 g
Salt	1/2 tsp.	2 mL
Freshly ground pepper, sprinkle		

Sauté leek, garlic and green pepper in olive oil and margarine in large pot or Dutch oven until leek is soft.

Add next 8 ingredients. Stir. Bring to a boil. Reduce heat. Cover. Simmer for 1 hour. Remove and discard bay leaf.

(continued on next page)

Stews

Add remaining 6 ingredients. Stir. Cover. Cook for 8 to 10 minutes. Makes 10 cups (2.5 L).

1 cup (250 mL): 198 Calories; 5.2 g Total Fat; 553 mg Sodium; 19 g Protein; 14 g Carbohydrate; 2 g Dietary Fiber

Pictured on page 35.

Easy Cioppino

An economical chup-PEE-noh (Italian fish stew) with a heady garlic and basil sauce. Serve with pasta on the side or crusty Italian bread for dipping. Delicious!

Medium onion, thinly sliced	1	1
Medium green pepper, slivered	1	1
Garlic clove, minced	1	1
Olive (or cooking) oil	2 tsp.	10 mL
Cans of stewed tomatoes (14 oz., 398 mL, each), with juice, broken up	2	2
Package of frozen cod fillets (or fresh), cubed	14 oz.	400 g
Uncooked medium shrimp (about 36), peeled and deveined	3/4 lb.	340 g
White (or alcohol-free) wine	1/4 cup	60 mL
Basil pesto	3 tbsp.	50 mL
Dried crushed chilies (optional)	1/8 tsp.	0.5 mL

Sauté onion, green pepper and garlic in olive oil in large frying pan until onion is soft.

Add stewed tomatoes with juice, cod, shrimp, wine, pesto and crushed chilies. Stir. Cover. Simmer for 3 to 5 minutes until fish flakes easily when tested with a fork and shrimp are pink and tails are curled slightly. Makes 6 1/2 cups (1.6 L).

1 cup (250 mL): 192 Calories; 5.1 g Total Fat; 448 mg Sodium; 23 g Protein; 12 g Carbohydrate; 2 g Dietary Fiber

Pictured on page 144 and back cover.

Seafood Gumbo

Traditional Louisiana browned-roux flavor. Rice adds thickness and texture.
You might even find this is better the next day.

Cooking oil	1/4 cup	60 mL
All-purpose flour	1/4 cup	60 mL
Hot water (see Note)	1 cup	250 mL
Can of diced tomatoes, with juice	28 oz.	796 mL
Fresh okra, chopped (or 2 boxes frozen, 8 oz., 250 g, each)	1 lb.	454 g
Water	4 cups	1 L
Chopped onion	1 cup	250 mL
Sliced celery	1/4 cup	60 mL
Diced green pepper	1/4 cup	60 mL
Cayenne pepper	1/4 - 1/2 tsp.	1 - 2 mL
Salt	1 tsp.	5 mL
Pepper	1/4 tsp.	1 mL
Garlic powder	1/4 tsp.	1 mL
Long grain white rice, uncooked	3/4 cup	175 mL
Medium cooked shrimp (about 48), peeled and deveined	1 lb.	454 g
Imitation crabmeat, cubed	1/2 lb.	225 g

Chopped green onion, for garnish

Stir cooking oil into flour in heavy saucepan on medium for about 10 minutes until flour turns dark brown in color.

Slowly stir in hot water. Mixture will steam. Heat and stir until thickened. Turn into large pot or Dutch oven.

Add next 10 ingredients. Bring to a boil. Reduce heat. Cover. Simmer for 1 hour.

Add rice. Simmer for 20 minutes until rice is tender.

Add shrimp and crab. Bring to a boil. Reduce heat. Simmer for 10 minutes.

Sprinkle green onion over individual servings. Makes 15 cups (3.74 L).

1 cup (250 mL): 151 Calories; 4.7 g Total Fat; 445 mg Sodium; 10 g Protein; 17 g Carbohydrate; 2 g Dietary Fiber

Note: Be sure to use hot water. Cold water will cause the roux to separate.

Stews

Caesar Stew

Rich flavor. Not too fishy. Clam tomato beverage works
very well as a seafood bouillon-type flavoring.

Medium onion, cut into 6 wedges	1	1
Sliced celery, with leaves	2/3 cup	150 mL
Garlic cloves, minced (or 3/4 tsp, 3 mL powder)	3	3
Olive (or cooking) oil	1 tbsp.	15 mL
Tomato clam cocktail	2 cups	500 mL
Can of diced tomatoes, with juice	14 oz.	398 mL
Small zucchini, cut into 1/4 inch (6 mm) slices	2	2
Baby carrots, halved	20	20
Lemon pepper	1/2 tsp.	2 mL
Celery seed	1/4 tsp.	1 mL
Vodka (or water)	1/4 cup	60 mL
Bluefish (or haddock or halibut), cubed	1 1/2 lbs.	680 g
Finely chopped fresh sweet basil (or 1 tsp., 5 mL, dried)	1 tbsp.	15 mL
Chopped fresh parsley	1/4 cup	60 mL
Whipping cream (or sour cream)	2 tbsp.	30 mL

Sauté onion, celery and garlic in olive oil in large pot or Dutch oven until onion is soft and golden.

Add next 7 ingredients. Bring to a boil. Reduce heat. Cover. Simmer for about 15 minutes until carrot is tender.

Add fish, basil and parsley. Stir. Cover. Simmer for about 10 minutes until fish flakes easily when tested with a fork. Remove fish and vegetables with slotted spoon to bowl. Keep warm. Simmer remaining liquid for about 10 minutes until reduced.

Gradually stir in whipping cream. Stir until heated through. Makes 8 cups (2 L).

1 cup (250 mL): 209 Calories; 6.9 g Total Fat; 410 mg Sodium; 19 g Protein; 14 g Carbohydrate;
1 g Dietary Fiber

St. Jacques Stew

Creamy, rich wine sauce with mild seafood flavor.

Leeks (white and tender parts only), thinly sliced	2	2
Garlic clove, minced (or 1/4 tsp., 1 mL, powder)	1	1
Sliced brown fresh mushrooms	2 cups	500 mL
Olive (or cooking) oil	1 tbsp.	15 mL
Water	2 cups	500 mL
Seafood (or chicken) bouillon powder	4 tsp.	20 mL
Unpeeled baby potatoes, cut in half	1 lb.	454 g
White (or alcohol-free) wine	1/3 cup	75 mL
Slivered red pepper, cut into 2 inch (5 cm) pieces	1/4 cup	60 mL
Salt	1/2 tsp.	2 mL
Dried thyme, crushed	1/4 tsp.	1 mL
Dried tarragon, crushed	1/8 tsp.	0.5 mL
Freshly ground pepper	1/8 tsp.	0.5 mL
Bay leaf	1	1
Fresh (or frozen) scallops, larger ones cut in half	1 lb.	454 g
Whipping cream	1/2 cup	125 mL
All-purpose flour	1 tbsp.	15 mL

Sauté leek, garlic and mushrooms in olive oil in large pot or Dutch oven until leek is soft and liquid from mushrooms has evaporated.

Add water, bouillon powder and potato. Stir. Cover. Simmer for 30 minutes until potato is tender.

Add next 7 ingredients. Stir. Bring to a boil.

Add scallops. Stir. Simmer, uncovered, for 5 to 6 minutes until scallops are firm but not tough.

Stir whipping cream into flour in small cup until smooth. Gradually stir into scallop mixture. Heat and stir until boiling and thickened. Makes 7 cups (1.75 L).

1 cup (250 mL): 223 Calories; 8.8 g Total Fat; 665 mg Sodium; 14 g Protein; 21 g Carbohydrate; 2 g Dietary Fiber

Pictured on page 53.

Vegetable Ragoût

Surprise—this stew is slightly sweet! Thick, pretty stew with a robust flavor.

Sliced fresh mushrooms	2 cups	500 mL
Diced onion	1 cup	250 mL
Garlic cloves, minced (or 3/4 tsp., 3 mL, powder)	3	3
Cooking oil	2 tsp.	10 mL
Water	3 cups	750 mL
Vegetable (or chicken) bouillon powder	1 tbsp.	15 mL
Long grain brown rice, uncooked	1/4 cup	60 mL
Wild rice, uncooked	1/4 cup	60 mL
Skim evaporated milk	1/2 cup	125 mL
Diced sweet potato	4 cups	1 L
Sliced carrot	2 cups	500 mL
Diced parsnips	1 cup	250 mL
Dried thyme	1 1/2 tsp.	7 mL
Salt	1/2 tsp.	2 mL
Pepper	1/8 tsp.	0.5 mL

Sauté mushrooms, onion, and garlic in cooking oil in large pot or Dutch oven until onion is soft and golden and mushrooms are browned.

Add water and bouillon powder. Stir. Bring to a boil. Add brown rice and wild rice. Stir. Reduce heat. Cover. Simmer for 35 minutes.

Add evaporated milk. Stir. Add remaining 6 ingredients. Stir. Cover. Simmer for 20 minutes until vegetables are soft and rice is tender. Makes 7 cups (1.75 L).

1 cup (250 mL): *214 Calories; 2.4 g Total Fat; 509 mg Sodium; 6 g Protein; 44 g Carbohydrate; 5 g Dietary Fiber*

Moroccan Stew

A colorful vegetable stew served over aromatic couscous.
Definite Middle-Eastern flavors—spicy and sweet.

Boiling water	1 cup	250 mL
Sun-dried tomato halves	1/4 cup	60 mL
Cubed potato	2 cups	500 mL
Sliced zucchini	2 cups	500 mL
Diced onion	1 1/2 cups	375 mL
Sliced carrot	1 1/2 cups	375 mL
Chopped green pepper	1 cup	250 mL
Olive (or cooking) oil	2 tbsp.	30 mL
Water	3 cups	750 mL
Can of chick peas (garbanzo beans), drained and rinsed	19 oz.	540 mL
Can of roasted red peppers, drained and slivered	14 oz.	398 mL
Raisins	1/4 cup	60 mL
Chicken (or vegetable) bouillon powder	1 tbsp.	15 mL
Ground ginger	1/2 tsp.	2 mL
Ground cinnamon	1/2 tsp.	2 mL
Turmeric	1/2 tsp.	2 mL
Salt	1/4 tsp.	1 mL
Cayenne pepper	1/4 tsp.	1 mL
Pepper	1/8 tsp.	0.5 mL
Water	1/3 cup	75 mL
Cornstarch	1 1/2 tbsp.	25 mL
CINNAMON COUSCOUS		
Water	2 cups	500 mL
Chicken (or vegetable) bouillon powder	1 tbsp.	15 mL
Hard margarine (or butter)	1 tbsp.	15 mL
Ground cinnamon	1/2 tsp.	2 mL
Couscous	1 1/2 cups	375 mL

(continued on next page)

Pour boiling water over sun-dried tomato in small bowl. Let stand for 15 minutes until softened. Drain. Cut into thin slivers. Set aside.

Sauté next 5 ingredients in olive oil in frying pan until vegetables are tender-crisp. Remove to large pot or Dutch oven.

Add next 11 ingredients. Add sun-dried tomato. Stir. Bring to a boil. Reduce heat. Cover. Simmer for about 25 minutes until vegetables are tender.

Stir water into cornstarch in small cup until smooth. Gradually stir into stew. Heat and stir until boiling and thickened. Makes 8 cups (2 L) stew.

Cinnamon Couscous: Combine water, bouillon, margarine and cinnamon in large saucepan. Bring to a boil. Add couscous. Stir. Remove from heat. Cover. Let stand for 10 minutes. Fluff with fork before serving. Makes 5 cups (1.25 L) couscous.

1 cup (250 mL) stew with couscous: 203 Calories; 4.1 g Total Fat; 625 mg Sodium; 6 g Protein; 36 g Carbohydrate; 3 g Dietary Fiber

Pictured on page 54.

 To dress up a soup or stew, dab a dollop of sour cream or yogurt in center of individual serving. Dip a knife into the dollop and drag to create swirls. Sprinkle with chives for a finishing touch.

Cassoulet

A hearty rich French stew that is traditionally cooked all day.
Using canned beans cuts the cooking time in half. Smells wonderful
and tastes great. Excellent choice.

Bacon slices, diced	6	6
All-purpose flour	1/2 cup	125 mL
Salt	1 tsp.	5 mL
Pepper	1/2 tsp.	2 mL
Lamb stew meat, trimmed of fat	1 1/2 lbs.	680 g
Pork stew meat, trimmed of fat	1 1/2 lbs.	680 g
Chopped onion	1 1/2 cups	375 mL
Garlic cloves, minced (or 1/2 tsp., 2 mL, powder)	2	2
White (or alcohol-free) wine	1/4 cup	60 mL
Can of tomato sauce	7 1/2 oz.	213 mL
Can of condensed chicken broth	10 oz.	284 mL
Dried thyme, crushed	1 tsp.	5 mL
Bay leaf	1	1
Cans of mixed beans (19 oz., 540 mL, each), drained and rinsed	2	2
Smoked ham sausage, cut into 1/2 inch (12 mm) slices	3/4 lb.	340 g
CROUTONS		
Hard margarine (or butter)	2 tbsp.	30 mL
Fresh white bread slices, cubed	3	3

Fry bacon in large frying pan until cooked, but not crisp. Remove with
slotted spoon to ungreased 4 quart (4 L) casserole or roaster.

Combine flour, salt and pepper in medium bowl or resealable plastic bag.
Dredge lamb and pork in flour mixture until well coated. Fry, in 3 to
4 batches, in bacon drippings in same frying pan until browned on all
sides. Remove with slotted spoon to casserole.

Sauté onion and garlic in same frying pan, adding wine, 1 tbsp. (15 mL) at
a time, as needed to scrape up brown bits from pan, until onion is soft.
Add to casserole.

Add any remaining wine, tomato sauce, broth, thyme, bay leaf, and beans.
Stir. Cover. Bake in 300°F (150°C) oven for 2 hours.

(continued on next page)

48 Stews

Add sausage. Stir.

Croutons: Heat margarine in large frying pan on medium-high until bubbling. Add bread cubes. Stir-fry for 10 minutes until crisp and browned. Scatter over top of casserole. Bake, uncovered, for 1 hour. Makes 11 cups (2.75 L).

1 cup (250 mL): 395 Calories; 15 g Total Fat; 1095 mg Sodium; 39 g Protein; 24 g Carbohydrate; 2 g Dietary Fiber

Chili-Sauced Pineapple Pork

The sweet pineapple taste is predominant but there's a wonderful lemon pepper and chili zip with some sweetness and some nip. Great served over wild rice.

All-purpose flour	3 tbsp.	50 mL
Chili powder	1 tsp.	5 mL
Lemon pepper	1 tsp.	5 mL
Boneless pork loin chops, thinly sliced into strips	1 lb.	454 g
Cooking oil	1 tbsp.	15 mL
Sliced carrot	1/2 cup	125 mL
Sliced celery	1/2 cup	125 mL
Small onion, sliced	1	1
Can of pineapple tidbits, with juice	14 oz.	398 mL
Chili sauce	1/4 cup	60 mL
Ketchup	1 tbsp.	15 mL
Brown sugar, packed	1 tbsp.	15 mL

Combine flour, chili powder and lemon pepper in medium bowl or resealable plastic bag. Dredge pork strips in flour mixture until well coated. Sear strips in cooking oil in large frying pan until browned. Remove with slotted spoon to small bowl.

Sauté carrot, celery and onion in same frying pan, scraping up any brown bits, until onion is soft.

Add pineapple with juice. Stir. Bring to a boil. Add chili sauce, ketchup and brown sugar. Stir. Add pork strips. Stir. Cover. Simmer for 30 minutes until pork is tender. Makes 4 1/2 cups (1.1 L).

1 cup (250 mL): 279 Calories; 8.4 g Total Fat; 119 mg Sodium; 24 g Protein; 27 g Carbohydrate; 2 g Dietary Fiber

Pictured on page 54.

Pork And Cabbage Stew

A subtle white wine flavor in the generous golden sauce.
Big pieces of meat and vegetables.

Boneless pork loin, cubed	1 1/2 lbs.	680 g
Mild Italian sausages, cut in half crosswise	3/4 lb.	340 g
Cooking oil	1 tbsp.	15 mL
Sliced carrot	4 cups	1 L
Large onion, cut into 8 wedges	1	1
Celery ribs, cut into 1 inch (2.5 cm) pieces	2	2
White (or alcohol-free) wine	1 cup	250 mL
Water	1/2 cup	125 mL
All-purpose flour	2 tbsp.	30 mL
Parsley flakes	2 tsp.	10 mL
Salt	1 tsp.	5 mL
Pepper	1/4 tsp.	1 mL
Bay leaf	1	1
Small head of cabbage, cut into 8 wedges	1	1

Sear pork and sausage in cooking oil in large pot or Dutch oven until browned on all sides.

Add next 10 ingredients. Stir. Reduce heat. Cover. Simmer for about 1 hour until pork is tender.

Arrange cabbage wedges in single layer in pinwheel formation over stew. Cover. Cook for 30 minutes until cabbage is tender-crisp. Carefully remove cabbage to form circle on large serving platter. Fill center of platter with stew. Remove and discard bay leaf. Makes 8 cups (2 L).

1 cup (250 mL): 371 Calories; 20.1 g Total Fat; 717 mg Sodium; 27 g Protein; 16 g Carbohydrate; 4 g Dietary Fiber

Pictured on page 36.

Black Bean Chili Stew

A complete-meal, casserole-type stew with a bit of a bite from the chilies.
The sauce thickens as it cools.

Lean pork stew meat, cubed	1 1/2 lbs.	680 g
Cooking oil	1 tbsp.	15 mL
Chopped onion	1/2 cup	125 mL
Garlic cloves, minced (or 1 tsp., 4 mL, powder), or less, if desired	4	4
Can of diced tomatoes, with juice	14 oz.	398 mL
Can of condensed cream of mushroom soup	10 oz.	284 mL
Cans of diced green chilies (4 oz., 114 mL, each), drained	2	2
Chunky-style salsa	1/2 cup	125 mL
Chicken bouillon powder	2 tsp.	10 mL
Ground cumin	1/2 tsp.	2 mL
Pepper	1/4 tsp.	1 mL
Long grain brown rice, uncooked	2/3 cup	150 mL
Can of black beans, drained and rinsed	19 oz.	540 mL

Sear pork in cooking oil in large frying pan until no longer pink. Remove to ungreased 3 quart (3 L) casserole.

Sauté onion and garlic in same frying pan, scraping up any brown bits, until onion is soft and golden. Add to pork.

Add next 7 ingredients to pork mixture. Cover. Bake in 325°F (160°C) oven for 1 hour.

Add brown rice and beans. Stir. Cover. Bake for 1 1/2 hours until rice is tender. Makes 8 cups (2 L).

1 cup (250 mL): 296 Calories; 9.2 g Total Fat; 719 mg Sodium; 24 g Protein; 29 g Carbohydrate;
2 g Dietary Fiber

Oktoberfest Pork

If you like the more sour taste of sauerkraut, you'll love this stew.

Pork shoulder roast, cubed	2 1/4 lbs.	1 kg
Kielbasa sausage, thinly sliced	6 oz.	170 g
Chopped onion	1 1/2 cups	375 mL
Water	3/4 cup	175 mL
Pepper	1/4 tsp.	1 mL
Sauerkraut, drained and rinsed	4 cups	1 L
White vinegar	1/3 cup	75 mL
Large potato, peeled and grated	1	1
Brown sugar, packed	2 tbsp.	30 mL
Caraway seed (optional)	1/4 tsp.	1 mL

Combine first 5 ingredients in greased 3 quart (3 L) casserole. Cover. Bake in 325°F (160°C) oven for 1 1/2 hours until pork is tender.

Add remaining 5 ingredients. Stir. Cover. Bake for 1 1/4 hours until bubbly and thickened. Makes 10 1/2 cups (2.6 L).

1 cup (250 mL): 292 Calories; 17.9 g Total Fat; 640 mg Sodium; 21 g Protein; 12 g Carbohydrate; 3 g Dietary Fiber

1. St. Jacques Stew, page 44
2. Dipping Sticks, page 140
3. Lentil Chowder, page 124

Props Courtesy Of: The Bay

Pork Stew With Gravy

A wonderful mellow flavor. A pork and gravy dinner all-in-one.

Boneless pork shoulder steak, trimmed of fat and cubed	1 1/2 lbs.	680 g
Cooking oil	2 tsp.	10 mL
Salt	1/2 tsp.	2 mL
Pepper	1/4 tsp.	1 mL
Medium potatoes, cubed	2	2
Medium carrots, sliced	2	2
Chopped onion	1 cup	250 mL
Frozen kernel corn	1 cup	250 mL
Can of condensed cream of mushroom soup	10 oz.	284 mL
Milk	1/2 cup	125 mL

Sear pork in cooking oil in frying pan until browned on all sides. Sprinkle with salt and pepper. Turn into ungreased 2 quart (2 L) casserole.

Add next 4 ingredients. Stir.

Combine soup and milk in small bowl. Stir well. Pour over pork mixture. Cover. Bake in 350°F (175°C) oven for about 1 1/2 hours until pork is very tender and vegetables are tender. Makes 6 cups (1.5 L).

1 cup (250 mL): 319 Calories; 14 g Total Fat; 715 mg Sodium; 26 g Protein; 23 g Carbohydrate; 2 g Dietary Fiber

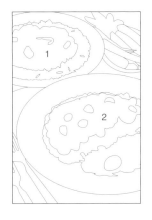

1. Chili-Sauced Pineapple Pork, page 49
2. Moroccan Stew, page 46

Props Courtesy Of: London Drugs

Stews

Sweet Pork And Apple Stew

A great stew to serve in the fall when the temperature is starting to cool off.
Serve over rice or mashed potatoes with a hearty crusty bread.

Pork shoulder steak, trimmed of fat and cubed	2 lbs.	900 g
Cooking oil	2 tsp.	10 mL
Baby carrots, halved	1 lb.	454 g
Vegetable cocktail juice (such as V8)	1 cup	250 mL
Small onions, quartered	2	2
Salt	1 tsp.	5 mL
Dried whole oregano	1/2 tsp.	2 mL
Paprika	1/4 tsp.	1 mL
Pepper	1/4 tsp.	1 mL
Ground rosemary	1/8 tsp.	0.5 mL
Medium cooking apples (such as MacIntosh or Golden Delicious), peeled, cored and cut into 8 wedges each	2	2
Vegetable cocktail juice (such as V8)	1/2 cup	125 mL
All-purpose flour	2 tbsp.	30 mL

Sear pork in cooking oil in large pot or Dutch oven until brown on all sides.

Add next 8 ingredients. Cover. Simmer for 45 minutes.

Add apple. Stir.

Stir second amount of juice into flour in small bowl until smooth. Gradually stir into stew. Cover. Heat for 20 minutes, stirring occasionally, until apples are tender and stew is thickened. Makes 8 cups (2 L).

1 cup (250 mL): 240 Calories; 9.7 g Total Fat; 578 mg Sodium; 23 g Protein; 15 g Carbohydrate; 1 g Dietary Fiber

Texas Chili

No beans in the traditional Texas chili. Serve with polenta or over pasta.

Beef inside round (or blade or chuck) steak, trimmed of fat and cubed	2 lbs.	900 g
Coarsely chopped onion	1 cup	250 mL
Garlic cloves, minced (or 1 tsp., 4 mL, powder)	4	4
Cooking oil	1 tbsp.	15 mL
Tomato juice	2 cups	500 mL
Can of condensed beef broth	10 oz.	284 mL
Paprika	1 tbsp.	15 mL
Dried whole oregano, crushed	2 tsp.	10 mL
Granulated sugar	2 tsp.	10 mL
Cumin seed, crushed	1 tsp.	5 mL
Salt	1 tsp.	5 mL
Dried crushed chilies	1/2 tsp.	2 mL
Ground allspice	1/2 tsp.	2 mL
Bay leaves	2	2
Yellow cornmeal	1/4 cup	60 mL

Sauté beef, onion and garlic in cooking oil in large pot or Dutch oven until beef is browned on all sides.

Add next 10 ingredients. Stir. Bring to a boil. Reduce heat. Cover. Simmer for 1 1/2 hours until beef is tender.

Add cornmeal. Stir. Cook, uncovered, for 20 to 30 minutes until thickened. Makes 5 3/4 cups (1.45 L).

1 cup (250 mL): 278 Calories; 6.5 g Total Fat; 1156 mg Sodium; 39 g Protein; 15 g Carbohydrate; 2 g Dietary Fiber

Rich Black Bean Chili

The bean flavor comes through, not too mild, not too spicy.

Dried black beans	1 lb.	454 g
Water		
Cold water	6 cups	1.5 L
Smoked pork hocks (or meaty ham bone)	1 lb.	454 g
Salt	1 tsp.	5 mL
Lean ground beef	1 1/2 lbs.	680 g
Garlic cloves, minced (or 3/4 tsp., 3 mL, powder)	3	3
Chopped onion	2 cups	500 mL
Cooking oil	2 tsp.	10 mL
Seasoned salt	1 tsp.	5 mL
Pepper	1/4 tsp.	1 mL
Diced carrot	1 cup	250 mL
Small green pepper, diced	1	1
Small red pepper, diced	1	1
Chili powder	4 tsp.	20 mL
Ground cumin	1/2 tsp.	2 mL
Hot pepper sauce	1/2 tsp.	2 mL

Sour cream, for garnish
Finely diced red onion, for garnish
Diced tomato, for garnish

Place beans in large saucepan. Cover with water by 2 inches (5 cm). Bring to a boil. Boil for 2 minutes. Turn off heat. Let stand for 1 hour. Drain. Turn into large pot or Dutch oven.

Add cold water and pork hocks. Bring to a boil. Cover. Boil slowly for 1 hour until beans are almost tender. Remove hocks. Cool enough to handle. Remove meat from bones and chop. Add meat to beans. Sprinkle with salt.

Scramble-fry ground beef, garlic and onion in cooking oil in large frying pan until beef is no longer pink. Drain. Sprinkle with seasoned salt and pepper. Add to bean mixture.

(continued on next page)

Chilies

Add next 6 ingredients. Cook, uncovered, for 30 minutes until carrot is tender.

Garnish individual servings with dollop of sour cream. Sprinkle with red onion and tomato. Makes 11 1/2 cups (2.9 L).

1 cup (250 mL): 293 Calories; 9.4 g Total Fat; 518 mg Sodium; 22 g Protein; 31 g Carbohydrate; 7 g Dietary Fiber

Pictured on page 90.

Chili With Barley

Tangy yet sweet. The barley adds a pleasant texture.

Lean ground beef	1 lb.	454 g
Chopped onion	1 cup	250 mL
Cooking oil	1 tsp.	5 mL
Chopped celery	1 cup	250 mL
Chopped green pepper	1 cup	250 mL
Chili powder	4 tsp.	20 mL
Salt	1 1/2 tsp.	7 mL
Ground cumin	1/4 tsp.	1 mL
Pepper	1/4 tsp.	1 mL
Cans of stewed tomatoes (14 oz., 398 mL, each), with juice	3	3
Water	1 cup	250 mL
Pearl barley	1/2 cup	125 mL

Scramble-fry ground beef and onion in cooking oil in large pot or Dutch oven. Drain.

Add next 6 ingredients. Stir. Cook for 5 minutes, stirring occasionally, until celery and green pepper are tender.

Add tomatoes with juice and water. Stir. Bring to a boil. Add barley. Stir. Cover. Simmer for 1 hour until barley is tender and chili is thickened. Makes 9 cups (2.25 L).

1 cup (250 mL): 178 Calories; 5.5 g Total Fat; 811 mg Sodium; 12 g Protein; 22 g Carbohydrate; 3 g Dietary Fiber

Chili And Stuffing

Mild chili that gets its pleasant blend of spices from the stuffing.
Can be chilled and brought out when ready to use. Really yummy!

Box of stove-top stuffing mix, prepared according to package directions	4 1/4 oz.	120 g
Lean ground beef	1/2 lb.	225 g
Chopped onion	1/2 cup	125 mL
Chopped celery	1/4 cup	60 mL
Cooking oil	1 tsp.	5 mL
Can of chili with beans	15 oz.	425 mL
Frozen kernel corn	1/2 cup	125 mL
Grated Monterey Jack cheese	1 cup	250 mL
Grated medium Cheddar cheese	1 cup	250 mL
Sliced ripe olives (optional)	1/4 cup	60 mL
Sour cream, for garnish	1/2 cup	125 mL

Pack stuffing into greased 2 quart (2 L) casserole.

Scramble-fry ground beef, onion and celery in cooking oil in large frying pan until beef is no longer pink. Drain.

Add chili with beans, corn and Monterey Jack cheese. Cook until bubbling. Pour over stuffing.

Sprinkle with Cheddar cheese and olives. Cover. Bake in 350°F (175°C) oven for 30 minutes.

Garnish individual servings with dollop of sour cream. Serves 4. Makes 4 3/4 cups (1.2 L).

1 cup (250 mL): 505 Calories; 27.3 g Total Fat; 1227 mg Sodium; 30 g Protein; 37 g Carbohydrate; 4 g Dietary Fiber

Pictured on page 89.

To Make Ahead: Prepare and assemble. Cover. Chill. Bake in 350°F (175°C) oven until heated through—1 hour if directly from refrigerator or 30 minutes if brought to room temperature.

Many Beans Chili Con Carne

Rich, spicy flavor. Filling and satisfying.

Lean ground beef	1 lb.	454 g
Chopped onion	1 1/2 cups	375 mL
Chopped celery	1 cup	250 mL
Garlic clove, minced (or 1/4 tsp., 1 mL, powder)	1	1
Chopped green pepper	1 1/3 cups	325 mL
Can of diced tomatoes, with juice	28 oz.	796 mL
Can of black beans, drained and rinsed	19 oz.	540 mL
Can of mixed beans, drained and rinsed	19 oz.	540 mL
Can of beans in tomato sauce	14 oz.	398 mL
Can of red kidney beans, drained and rinsed	14 oz.	398 mL
Can of condensed tomato soup	10 oz.	284 mL
Granulated sugar	3 tbsp.	50 mL
Chili powder	2 tbsp.	30 mL
Cayenne pepper	1/2 - 1 tsp.	2 - 5 mL
Ground cumin	1/2 - 1 tsp.	2 - 5 mL

Scramble-fry ground beef, onion, celery, garlic and green pepper in large pot or Dutch oven until beef is no longer pink. Drain.

Add remaining 10 ingredients. Stir well. Bring to a boil. Reduce heat to medium-low. Simmer for 45 minutes, stirring every 15 minutes.
Makes 12 cups (3 L).

1 cup (250 mL): 234 Calories; 4.7 g Total Fat; 614 mg Sodium; 15 g Protein; 35 g Carbohydrate; 6 g Dietary Fiber

 tip   *Corn and taco chips, either left whole or crushed, make a tasty topping for chili.*

Oriental Chili

Spicy with tender beef and crunchy bean sprouts.
Serve over rice or vermicelli noodles.

Flank steak, very thinly sliced on diagonal	1 lb.	454 g
Cooking oil	1 tbsp.	15 mL
Freshly grated gingerroot	1 tbsp.	15 mL
Garlic cloves, minced (or 3/4 tsp., 3 mL powder)	3	3
Medium onion, cut lengthwise into wedges	1	1
Medium green pepper, slivered	1	1
Medium carrot, thinly sliced on diagonal	1	1
Can of diced tomatoes, with juice	14 oz.	398 mL
Can of black beans, drained and rinsed	19 oz.	540 mL
Hoisin sauce	2 tbsp.	30 mL
Ground fresh chili paste (available in Asian section of grocery store)	1 tbsp.	15 mL
Soy sauce	2 tbsp.	30 mL
Sherry (or alcohol-free sherry)	1/4 cup	60 mL
Fresh bean sprouts (large handful)	6 oz.	170 g

Sauté beef in cooking oil in large pot or Dutch oven until just browned. Add ginger, garlic, onion, green pepper and carrot. Sauté until vegetables are soft.

Add tomatoes with juice and beans. Stir.

Combine hoisin sauce, chili purée, soy sauce and sherry in small bowl. Add to beef mixture. Stir. Simmer, uncovered, for 30 minutes, stirring occasionally.

Add bean sprouts. Heat and stir on medium until boiling and thickened. Bean sprouts should still be crisp. Makes 8 cups (2 L).

1 cup (250 mL): 202 Calories; 6.4 g Total Fat; 635 mg Sodium; 17 g Protein; 18 g Carbohydrate; 1 g Dietary Fiber

Chunky Chili

The sausage meat adds such a nice flavor. Just enough bite.

Sirloin steak, trimmed of fat and cubed	1 1/2 lbs.	680 g
Pork sausage meat	1 lb.	454 g
Garlic clove, crushed (or 1/4 tsp., 1 mL, powder)	1	1
Finely chopped onion	3/4 cup	175 mL
Finely chopped celery	1/2 cup	125 mL
Cans of red kidney beans (14 oz., 398 mL, each), drained and rinsed	2	2
Can of crushed tomatoes	14 oz.	398 mL
Water	1/2 cup	125 mL
Apple cider vinegar	1 tbsp.	15 mL
Chili powder	4 tsp.	20 mL
Celery salt	1 tsp.	5 mL
Cayenne pepper	1/4 tsp.	1 mL

Sauté beef and sausage meat in large non-stick frying pan until beef is no longer pink. Drain well.

Add garlic, onion and celery. Sauté until onion is soft.

Add remaining 7 ingredients. Stir. Cover. Simmer on low for 1 hour until thickened. Makes 8 cups (2 L).

1 cup (250 mL): 263 Calories; 9.3 g Total Fat; 631 mg Sodium; 27 g Protein; 19 g Carbohydrate;

Paré Pointer

He decided to become an astronaut after being told repeatedly that he was no earthly good.

Chili-Stuffed Peppers

Tastes as good as it looks.

Lean ground beef	1/2 lb.	225 g
Chopped onion	1 cup	250 mL
Garlic cloves, minced (or 1/2 tsp., 2 mL, powder)	2	2
Cooking oil	2 tsp.	10 mL
Water	1 cup	250 mL
Brown rice, uncooked	1/2 cup	125 mL
Can of red kidney beans, drained, rinsed and coarsely mashed	14 oz.	398 mL
Can of tomato paste	5 1/2 oz.	156 mL
Chili powder	2 tsp.	10 mL
Granulated sugar	1 tsp.	5 mL
Ground cumin	1/2 tsp.	2 mL
Salt	1/2 tsp.	2 mL
Large green, red or yellow peppers	4	4
Boiling water	12 cups	3 L
Grated sharp Cheddar cheese	3/4 cup	175 mL
Grated Monterey Jack cheese	3/4 cup	175 mL

Scramble-fry ground beef, onion and garlic in cooking oil in large pot or Dutch oven until beef is no longer pink.

Add water and brown rice. Stir. Bring to a boil. Cover. Cook for 30 minutes until rice is almost tender.

Add beans, tomato paste, chili powder, sugar, cumin and salt. Stir. Simmer, uncovered, for about 10 minutes to allow flavors to blend.

Cut peppers in half lengthwise through stem. Remove seeds, leaving stem intact. Blanch in boiling water in large pot or Dutch oven for 2 minutes. Drain. Rinse under cold water. Drain. Blot insides with paper towel. Fill peppers with chili.

(continued on next page)

Combine both cheeses in small bowl. Sprinkle cheese on peppers. Place on baking sheet. Broil on center rack in oven for about 10 minutes until cheese is melted and peppers are hot. Makes 8 stuffed pepper halves.

1 stuffed pepper half: 292 Calories; 13.5 g Total Fat; 387 mg Sodium; 16 g Protein; 28 g Carbohydrate; 5 g Dietary Fiber

Pictured on page 71.

Southwest Chili Hash

An easy one-dish meal with just the right amount of spice.

Lean ground beef	1 lb.	454 g
Chopped onion	1 cup	250 mL
Chopped celery	1 cup	250 mL
Can of crushed tomatoes	14 oz.	398 mL
Can of stewed tomatoes, with juice, broken up	14 oz.	398 mL
Water	1 1/2 cups	375 mL
Long grain white rice, uncooked	1 cup	250 mL
Chili powder	2 tsp. - 1 tbsp.	10 - 15 mL
Salt	1 tsp.	5 mL
Pepper	1/4 tsp.	1 mL

Scramble-fry ground beef, onion and celery in large non-stick frying pan until beef is no longer pink. Drain. Turn into greased 3 quart (3 L) casserole.

Add remaining 7 ingredients. Stir. Cover. Bake in 375°F (190°C) oven for about 1 hour until rice is tender. Makes 8 cups (2 L).

1 cup (250 mL): 213 Calories; 5.4 g Total Fat; 561 mg Sodium; 13 g Protein; 28 g Carbohydrate; 2 g Dietary Fiber

 Instead of eating chili with bread or taco chips, try celery sticks. They are great dippers because of their crunch and fresh flavor.

Cowboy Calzones

A hand-held lunch for a hungry hard worker. Uses leftover roast beef.
These cal-ZOH-nays are great.

Chopped onion	1/2 cup	125 mL
Cooking oil	2 tsp.	10 mL
All-purpose flour	1 tbsp.	15 mL
Chili powder	2 tsp.	10 mL
Chili sauce	2 tbsp.	30 mL
Can of pork and beans with tomato sauce	14 oz.	398 mL
Fine bread crumbs	3 tbsp.	50 mL
Finely chopped cooked roast beef	1 cup	250 mL
Grated sharp Cheddar cheese	1 cup	250 mL
Frozen whole wheat bread dough (1 lb., 454 g, each), thawed	2	2

Sauté onion in cooking oil in medium frying pan until soft.

Sprinkle with flour and chili powder. Stir well. Add chili sauce, pork and beans and bread crumbs. Stir. Heat, stirring occasionally, until simmering and thickened. Remove from heat.

Add beef and cheese. Stir. Makes 3 1/2 cups (875 mL) filling. Cool slightly.

Place dough on lightly floured surface. Cut each loaf into 5 portions. Roll out each portion to 8 inch (20 cm) circle. Spread 1/2 of circle with scant 1/3 cup (75 mL) filling. Moisten entire edge with water. Fold dough and press to seal, folding edge upward and over. Crimp edge with fork. Repeat with remaining dough and filling. Make X slit with sharp knife on top. Place on greased baking sheet. Bake in 375°F (190°C) oven for 15 to 18 minutes. Makes 10 calzones.

1 calzone: 363 Calories; 10.2 g Total Fat; 774 mg Sodium; 19 g Protein; 54 g Carbohydrate; 9 g Dietary Fiber

Chili Burritos

A nice change from the usual hamburger.

Boneless inside round (or blade or chuck) steak, trimmed of fat	1/2 lb.	225 g
Medium onion, cut into 6 wedges	1	1
Garlic cloves, minced (or 1/2 tsp., 2 mL, powder)	2	2
Cooking oil	2 tsp.	10 mL
Sliced fresh mushrooms	1 cup	250 mL
Chili powder	1 tsp.	5 mL
Ground cumin	1/4 tsp.	1 mL
Can of red kidney beans, drained, rinsed and coarsely mashed	14 oz.	398 mL
Can of tomato sauce	7 1/2 oz.	213 mL
Dried whole oregano, crushed	1/2 tsp.	2 mL
Granulated sugar	1/4 tsp.	1 mL
Pepper	1/8 tsp.	0.5 mL
Whole wheat (or tomato) flour tortillas (8 inch, 20 cm, size), warmed	6	6

Cut steak into 6 pieces. Place in food processor. Pulse several times until coarsely chopped.

Add onion and garlic. Pulse several times until finely chopped but not puréed.

Sauté beef mixture in cooking oil in large frying pan until no longer pink.

Add mushrooms, chili powder and cumin. Stir. Cook until mushrooms are soft.

Add next 5 ingredients. Simmer, uncovered, for 10 minutes until thickened. Makes 3 cups (750 mL) filling.

Place 1/2 cup (125 mL) filling in center of each tortilla. Fold envelope style, tucking in sides. Makes 6 burritos.

1 burrito: 245 Calories; 5.3 g Total Fat; 506 mg Sodium; 16 g Protein; 34 g Carbohydrate; 5 g Dietary Fiber

Chili Nachos

A dry chili that covers tortilla chips well. A trendy way to serve chili.

Extra lean ground beef	8 oz.	225 g
Can of red kidney beans, drained and rinsed	14 oz.	398 mL
Chopped celery	1/2 cup	125 mL
Chopped onion	1/2 cup	125 mL
Medium tomato, seeded and diced	1	1
Chili powder	2 tsp.	10 mL
Paprika	1 tsp.	5 mL
Salt	1/2 tsp.	2 mL
Dried crushed chilies	1/8 tsp.	0.5 mL
Pepper, sprinkle		
Water, if necessary	1 - 2 tbsp.	15 - 30 mL
Tortilla chips	5 oz.	140 g
Grated Monterey Jack cheese	3/4 cup	175 mL
Grated medium Cheddar cheese	3/4 cup	175 mL
Chopped and seeded jalapeño pepper (optional), see Note	2 tbsp.	30 mL

Scramble-fry ground beef in large non-stick frying pan until no longer pink. Drain.

Add next 9 ingredients. Stir.

Heat on medium-low for 20 minutes, stirring occasionally, adding water, 1 tbsp. (15 mL) at a time, as necessary to keep from burning. Mixture should be dry enough to sprinkle.

Arrange layer of tortilla chips on greased foil-lined 11 x 17 inch (28 x 43 cm) baking sheet. Sprinkle with Monterey Jack cheese. Cover with chili mixture. Sprinkle with Cheddar cheese and jalapeño pepper. Bake, uncovered, in 400°F (205°C) oven for 10 minutes until cheese is melted. Serves 8.

1 serving: 265 Calories; 14.5 g Total Fat; 467 mg Sodium; 15 g Protein; 20 g Carbohydrate; 4 g Dietary Fiber

Note: Wear gloves when chopping jalapeño peppers and avoid touching your eyes.

Chilies

Cheesy Chili Pasta

A quick top-of-the-stove meal.

Lean ground beef	1 lb.	454 g
Garlic clove, minced (or 1/4 tsp., 1 mL, powder)	1	1
Chopped onion	1 cup	250 mL
Chopped celery	1/2 cup	125 mL
Cooking oil	1 tsp.	5 mL
Can of Italian-style stewed tomatoes, with juice	19 oz.	540 mL
Chili sauce	1/2 cup	125 mL
Chili powder (or more to taste)	1 tsp.	5 mL
Water	1 cup	250 mL
Tiny pasta shells	1 1/2 cups	375 mL
Grated medium Cheddar cheese	2 cups	500 mL

Scramble-fry ground beef, garlic, onion and celery in cooking oil in large frying pan until beef is no longer pink. Drain.

Add tomatoes with juice, chili sauce, chili powder and water. Stir. Bring to a boil. Add pasta. Stir. Cover. Simmer for 15 to 20 minutes, stirring occasionally, until pasta is tender but firm and liquid is mostly absorbed.

Add cheese. Heat and stir until melted. Makes 6 cups (1.5 L).

1 cup (250 mL): 430 Calories; 21.3 g Total Fat; 554 mg Sodium; 28 g Protein; 32 g Carbohydrate; 3 g Dietary Fiber

Pictured on page 89.

Chilies

Chili-Go-Quickly

Only seven ingredients and four of them come right from the pantry.

Lean ground beef	1 lb.	454 g
Envelope of taco seasoning mix	1 1/4 oz.	35 g
All-purpose flour	1 tbsp.	15 mL
Can of stewed tomatoes, with juice, broken up	14 oz.	398 mL
Tomato juice	1 cup	250 mL
Can of red kidney beans, drained and rinsed	14 oz.	398 mL
Can of pork and beans in tomato sauce	14 oz.	398 mL

Scramble-fry ground beef in large non-stick frying pan until no longer pink. Drain.

Sprinkle with taco seasoning mix and flour. Mix well. Add tomatoes with juice and tomato juice. Stir. Heat for about 25 minutes until bubbling and thickened.

Add kidney beans and pork and beans in tomato sauce. Stir. Simmer for 10 minutes, stirring occasionally. Makes 6 1/2 cups (1.6 L).

1 cup (250 mL): 257 Calories; 7.2 g Total Fat; 1326 mg Sodium; 20 g Protein; 30 g Carbohydrate; 7 g Dietary Fiber

1. Pepper Cheese Bread, page 132
2. Chili-Stuffed Peppers, page 64
3. Pork Meatball Chili, page 96

Props Courtesy Of:
Alberta Craft Council Craft Gallery Shop

One-Step Chili Dinner

Why buy packaged "helpers" with all those additives when you can make this recipe every bit as easily from your kitchen cupboard.

Lean ground beef	1 lb.	454 g
Onion flakes	1 tbsp.	15 mL
Celery salt	1 tsp.	5 mL
Chili powder	1 1/2 tsp.	7 mL
Pepper	1/8 tsp.	0.5 mL
Can of condensed tomato soup	10 oz.	284 mL
Frozen kernel corn	2/3 cup	150 mL
Diced green pepper	1/3 cup	75 mL
Hot water	3 cups	750 mL
Medium egg noodles, uncooked	1 1/2 cups	375 mL

Scramble-fry ground beef in large non-stick frying pan until no longer pink. Drain.

Sprinkle with onion flakes, celery salt, chili powder and pepper. Mix well. Add soup, corn, green pepper and hot water. Stir. Bring to a boil.

Add egg noodles. Stir. Cover. Simmer for about 10 minutes, stirring occasionally, until noodles are tender but firm. Remove from heat. Let stand for 30 to 40 minutes until liquid is absorbed. Makes 6 cups (1.5 L).

1 cup (250 mL): 213 Calories; 8 g Total Fat; 595 mg Sodium; 17 g Protein; 20 g Carbohydrate; 1 g Dietary Fiber

1. Bulgur Chili, page 94
2. Sliced Pickled Peppers, page 147
3. Summer Vegetable Chili, page 86

Props Courtesy Of: Stokes
The Bay

Chilies

Stove-Top Chili Pasta

A serve-from-the-saucepan meal.

Lean ground beef	1 lb.	454 g
Chopped onion	3/4 cup	175 mL
Can of diced tomatoes, with juice	28 oz.	796 mL
Can of red kidney beans, drained and rinsed	19 oz.	540 mL
Water	2 cups	500 mL
Chili powder	3 - 4 tsp.	15 - 20 mL
Granulated sugar	1 tsp.	5 mL
Salt	1 1/2 tsp.	7 mL
Pepper	1/4 tsp.	1 mL
Penne pasta	1 1/2 cups	375 mL
Grated Parmesan cheese	1/4 cup	60 mL

Scramble-fry ground beef and onion in large pot or Dutch oven until beef is no longer pink. Drain.

Add next 7 ingredients. Stir. Bring to a boil.

Add pasta. Stir. Cover. Simmer for about 10 minutes, stirring frequently, until pasta is almost cooked. Remove cover. Simmer until pasta is tender but firm and sauce is mostly absorbed.

Add Parmesan cheese. Stir. Makes 8 cups (2 L).

1 cup (250 mL): 220 Calories; 6.7 g Total Fat; 788 mg Sodium; 17 g Protein; 24 g Carbohydrate; 4 g Dietary Fiber

Paré Pointer

When the weatherman said the moon was down to its last quarter, Johnny wanted to send some money to help out.

Chilies

Turkey Chili With Basil

Swirl in a dollop of yogurt to cool the taste buds. Wonderful flavors.

Salt	1 tsp.	5 mL
Lemon pepper	1 tsp.	5 mL
Ground white turkey breast	1 lb.	454 g
Olive (or cooking) oil	1 tbsp.	15 mL
Chopped onion	1 1/2 cups	375 mL
Diced celery	1 1/2 cups	375 mL
Garlic cloves, minced (or 1/2 tsp., 2 mL, powder)	2	2
Can of white kidney (cannellini) beans, drained and rinsed	19 oz.	540 mL
Can of diced tomatoes, with juice	14 oz.	398 mL
Diced green pepper	1 1/2 cups	375 mL
Chili sauce	1/2 cup	125 mL
Chopped fresh parsley	1/4 cup	60 mL
White (or alcohol-free) wine	3 tbsp.	50 mL
Chili powder	1 tbsp.	15 mL
Dried sweet basil	2 tsp.	10 mL
Granulated sugar	1 tsp.	5 mL
Ground cumin	1/4 tsp.	1 mL
Cayenne pepper	1/8 tsp.	0.5 mL
Jalapeño pepper, seeded and finely diced (see Note)	1	1

Sprinkle salt and lemon pepper over ground turkey. Scramble-fry in olive oil in large frying pan until turkey is no longer pink. Remove with slotted spoon to ungreased 3 quart (3 L) casserole.

Sauté onion, celery and garlic in same frying pan until onion is soft. Add to turkey.

Add remaining 12 ingredients. Stir. Bake, uncovered, in 350°F (175°C) oven for 45 minutes, stirring twice, until thickened. Makes 8 cups (2 L).

1 cup (250 mL): 171 Calories; 2.8 g Total Fat; 520 mg Sodium; 19 g Protein; 18 g Carbohydrate; 2 g Dietary Fiber

Note: Wear gloves when chopping jalapeño peppers and avoid touching your eyes.

Chilies

Chili Wraps

They might be messy, but they sure do taste good.
Colorful stuffing showing in the end of each.

Long grain white rice (see Note)	1 cup	250 mL
Boiling water	2 cups	500 mL
Salt	1 tsp.	5 mL
Lean ground chicken (about 1 1/4 cups, 300 mL)	3/4 lb.	340 g
Cooking oil	1 tsp.	5 mL
Chopped green onion	1 cup	250 mL
Medium tomatoes (about 4 1/2 cups, 1.1 L), diced	4	4
Can of chili beans, with spices	14 oz.	398 mL
Small green jalapeño pepper, seeded and diced (see Note)	1	1
Chopped fresh cilantro (optional)	1/4 cup	60 mL
Flour tortillas (10 inch, 25 cm, size), warmed	6	6
Medium carrot, grated	1	1
Diced green pepper	1/2 cup	125 mL
Diced red onion	1/3 cup	75 mL
Grated sharp Cheddar cheese	1 cup	250 mL
Salsa	1/2 cup	125 mL

Cook rice in boiling water and salt in large covered saucepan for about 20 minutes until tender and water is absorbed. Fluff with fork. Set aside.

Scramble-fry ground chicken in cooking oil in large frying pan until no longer pink. Drain.

Add green onion. Stir. Cook for 2 minutes.

Add tomato, chili beans and jalapeño pepper. Simmer, uncovered, for 15 to 20 minutes until thickened.

Add cilantro. Cook for 2 minutes.

Spoon 1/2 cup (125 mL) rice onto center of tortilla. Spoon 1/2 cup (125 mL) chili mixture onto rice. Sprinkle with 1/6 of carrot, green pepper, red onion and cheese. Add a dab of salsa. Fold tortilla around filling, tucking in sides. Repeat with remaining tortillas and filling. Makes 6 wraps.

(continued on next page)

Chilies

1 wrap: *525 Calories; 20 g Total Fat; 1162 mg Sodium; 23 g Protein; 64 g Carbohydrate;*
7 g Dietary Fiber

Note: Regular long grain white rice is recommended because it will be sticky when prepared and this is what is preferred for this recipe. Converted rice doesn't stick together as well.

Note: Wear gloves when chopping jalapeño peppers and avoid touching your eyes.

Sweet Pumpkin Chili

The pumpkin makes this thick sauce rich-tasting with an unusual flavor.

Lean ground chicken	1 1/2 lbs.	680 g
Chopped onion	1 cup	250 mL
Sliced celery	1/2 cup	125 mL
Garlic clove, minced (or 1/4 tsp., 1 mL, powder), optional	1	1
Cooking oil	1 tbsp.	15 mL
Can of stewed tomatoes, with juice	28 oz.	796 mL
Can of chick peas (garbanzo beans), drained and rinsed	14 oz.	398 mL
Can of pumpkin (without spices)	14 oz.	398 mL
Can of Romano beans, drained and rinsed	14 oz.	398 mL
Brown sugar, packed	1 tbsp.	15 mL
Chili powder	1 tbsp.	15 mL
Ground cinnamon	1 tsp.	5 mL
Salt	1/2 tsp.	2 mL
Dried crushed chilies	1/8 tsp.	0.5 mL
Ground cloves	1/8 tsp.	0.5 mL

Scramble-fry ground chicken, onion, celery and garlic in cooking oil in large pot or Dutch oven until chicken is no longer pink.

Add next 10 ingredients. Stir. Cover. Simmer for about 45 minutes, stirring frequently. Makes 10 cups (2.5 L).

1 cup (250 mL): *262 Calories; 11.6 g Total Fat; 499 mg Sodium; 17 g Protein; 24 g Carbohydrate;*
3 g Dietary Fiber

 tip   *When the family carves pumpkins at Halloween, save the pulp for use in recipes. Cook in a small amount of water in a covered saucepan until soft. Drain and mash. Freeze in resealable plastic bags.*

Chilies

California Chili

Topped with an avocado yogurt raita (RI-tah) that's incredibly good.

Boneless, skinless chicken breast halves (about 2), cut into strips	1/2 lb.	225 g
Jalapeño pepper, seeded and finely diced (see Note)	1	1
Olive (or cooking) oil	1 tbsp.	15 mL
Diced plum tomato	2 cups	500 mL
Chopped red onion	1 cup	250 mL
Diced red pepper	1 cup	250 mL
Chopped fresh sweet basil	2 tbsp.	30 mL
Garlic cloves, minced (or 3/4 tsp., 3 mL powder)	3	3
Chili powder	2 tsp.	10 mL
Freshly ground pepper	1 tsp.	5 mL
Salt	1 tsp.	5 mL
Ground cumin	1/2 tsp.	2 mL
Ground coriander	1/4 tsp.	1 mL
AVOCADO YOGURT RAITA		
Ripe avocado, diced	1	1
Prepared orange juice	1 tbsp.	15 mL
Plain yogurt	1 cup	250 mL
Chopped fresh parsley (or cilantro)	1/4 cup	60 mL

Toasted shelled sunflower seeds (optional)

Sauté chicken and jalapeño pepper in olive oil in large frying pan until chicken is no longer pink.

Add next 10 ingredients. Stir. Cook for 15 minutes on medium-high until vegetables are tender-crisp. Makes 5 1/2 cups (1.4 L) chili.

Avocado Yogurt Raita: Combine first 4 ingredients in small bowl. Let stand for 10 minutes to allow flavors to blend. Makes 1 2/3 cups (400 mL) raita. Spoon 1/4 cup (60 mL) onto individual servings.

Sprinkle with sunflower seeds. Makes about 7 cups (1.75 L).

(continued on next page)

Chilies

1 cup (250 mL): 253 Calories; 13.4 g Total Fat; 532 mg Sodium; 16 g Protein; 21 g Carbohydrate; 4 g Dietary Fiber

Note: Wear gloves when chopping jalapeño peppers and avoid touching your eyes.

CALIFORNIA CHILI WRAPS: Use 1/2 cup (125 mL) filling and a dab of raita for each 10 inch (25 cm) flour tortilla. Makes 11 wraps.

Cashew Chicken Chili

An unusual, mild-flavored chili. Great served over rice.

Boneless, skinless chicken breast halves (about 6), cut into thin strips	1 1/2 lbs.	680 g
Olive (or cooking) oil	2 tsp.	10 mL
Sliced fresh mushrooms	2 cups	500 mL
Chopped onion	1 1/2 cups	375 mL
Diced red pepper	1 cup	250 mL
Garlic clove, minced (or 1/4 tsp., 1 mL, powder)	1	1
Can of white kidney (cannellini) beans, drained and rinsed	19 oz.	540 mL
Can of cream-style corn	14 oz.	398 mL
Frozen peas	1 cup	250 mL
Chili powder	2 tsp.	10 mL
Salt	1/4 tsp.	1 mL
Pepper	1/8 tsp.	0.5 mL
Chopped salted cashews	1/2 cup	125 mL

Sauté chicken in olive oil in large frying pan until no longer pink.

Add next 4 ingredients. Stir. Cook on medium for about 10 minutes until liquid is absorbed.

Add beans, corn, peas, chili powder, salt and pepper. Stir. Simmer, uncovered, for 15 minutes, stirring occasionally.

Sprinkle cashews over individual servings. Makes 6 1/2 cups (1.6 L).

1 cup (250 mL): 338 Calories; 9.2 g Total Fat; 535 mg Sodium; 32 g Protein; 34 g Carbohydrate; 3 g Dietary Fiber

Chilies

Creamy White Chili

Serve with a hearty bread or Pumpkin Corn Cakes, page 142.

Boneless, skinless chicken breast halves (about 6), diced	1 1/2 lbs.	680 g
Chopped onion	1 cup	250 mL
Thinly sliced celery (use white part only)	1 cup	250 mL
Garlic cloves, minced (or 1/2 tsp., 2 mL, powder)	2	2
Cooking oil	2 tbsp.	30 mL
Cans of white kidney (cannellini) beans (19 oz., 540 mL, each), drained and rinsed	2	2
Can of peaches and cream kernel corn, with liquid	12 oz.	341 mL
Sliced fresh mushrooms	1 cup	250 mL
Julienned yellow zucchini, with peel (see Tip, page 25)	1 cup	250 mL
Cans of diced green chilies (4 oz., 114 mL, each), with liquid	2	2
Chicken bouillon powder	2 tsp.	10 mL
Ground cumin	1 tsp.	5 mL
Ground coriander	1/2 tsp.	2 mL
White pepper	1/2 tsp.	2 mL
Half-and-half cream	1 cup	250 mL
All-purpose flour	1 tbsp.	15 mL
Grated Monterey Jack with Jalapeño cheese	1 cup	250 mL
Grated Monterey Jack cheese, for garnish	3 tbsp.	50 mL
Chopped fresh parsley (or cilantro), for garnish	2 tbsp.	30 mL

Sauté chicken, onion, celery and garlic in cooking oil in large Dutch oven or frying pan until chicken is no longer pink and onion is soft.

Add next 9 ingredients. Stir. Cover. Simmer for 40 minutes, stirring occasionally.

(continued on next page)

Chilies

Stir cream into flour in small bowl until smooth. Stir into chili. Add first amount of cheese. Heat and stir until thickened and heated through.

Sprinkle second amount cheese and parsley over individual servings. Makes 9 cups (2.25 L).

1 cup (250 mL): 329 Calories; 12.6 g Total Fat; 1115 mg Sodium; 28 g Protein; 28 g Carbohydrate; 1 g Dietary Fiber

Pictured on page 90.

Lima Chicken Chili

A creamy, mild chili made from canned goods in your cupboard.

Lean ground chicken (or turkey)	1 1/2 lbs.	680 g
Chopped onion	1 cup	250 mL
Diced red pepper	1/2 cup	125 mL
Cooking oil	2 tsp.	10 mL
Chili powder	4 tsp.	20 mL
Garlic salt (or salt)	1 tsp.	5 mL
Granulated sugar	1 tsp.	5 mL
Celery seed	1/2 tsp.	2 mL
Dried savory leaves, crushed	1/8 tsp.	0.5 mL
Pepper	1/8 tsp.	0.5 mL
Cans of diced tomatoes (14 oz., 398 mL, each)	2	2
Cans of lima beans (14 oz., 398 mL, each), drained and rinsed	2	2
Cans of kernel corn (12 oz., 341 mL, each), drained	2	2
Can of condensed cream of mushroom soup	10 oz.	284 mL

Scramble-fry ground chicken, onion and red pepper in cooking oil in large pot or Dutch oven until chicken is no longer pink.

Add next 6 ingredients. Stir. Cook for 5 minutes, stirring frequently.

Add remaining 4 ingredients. Stir. Cover. Simmer on low for 1 hour, stirring occasionally to prevent scorching. Makes 12 cups (3 L).

1 cup (250 mL): 245 Calories; 11.2 g Total Fat; 661 mg Sodium; 15 g Protein; 23 g Carbohydrate; 2 g Dietary Fiber

Chicken And Lentil Chili

The lentils give a slightly different flavor than the usual chili.

Lean ground chicken	1 lb.	454 g
Chopped onion	1/2 cup	125 mL
Chopped celery	1/2 cup	125 mL
Garlic clove, minced (or 1/4 tsp., 1 mL, powder)	1	1
Chopped green pepper	1 cup	250 mL
Jalapeño pepper, seeds removed and diced (see Note)	1	1
Cooking oil	2 tsp.	10 mL
Water	4 cups	1 L
Brown lentils	1 cup	250 mL
Bay leaf	1	1
Can of diced tomatoes, with juice	28 oz.	796 mL
Diced potato	1 1/2 cups	375 mL
Chili powder	1 tbsp.	15 mL
Dried whole oregano	1 tsp.	5 mL
Hot pepper sauce	1/2 tsp.	2 mL
Salt	1/2 tsp.	2 mL
Pepper	1/2 tsp.	2 mL

Scramble-fry ground chicken, onion, celery, garlic, green pepper and jalapeño pepper in cooking oil in large pot or Dutch oven until chicken is no longer pink.

Add water. Bring to a boil. Add lentils and bay leaf. Reduce heat to medium-low. Cover. Simmer for 40 minutes. Remove and discard bay leaf.

Add remaining 7 ingredients. Simmer, uncovered, for 45 minutes until thickened and potato is tender. Makes 8 cups (2 L).

1 cup (250 mL): 268 Calories; 9.6 g Total Fat; 378 mg Sodium; 19 g Protein; 28 g Carbohydrate; 5 g Dietary Fiber

Note: Wear gloves when chopping jalapeño peppers and avoid touching your eyes.

Chicken And Pepper Chili

This is a great potluck recipe that is a bit different than the usual.

Lean ground chicken	1 lb.	454 g
Diced red onion	2 cups	500 mL
Fresh jalapeño peppers, seeds removed and diced (see Note)	2	2
Olive (or cooking) oil	2 tsp.	10 mL
Can of diced tomatoes, with juice	28 oz.	796 mL
Can of black beans, drained and rinsed	19 oz.	540 mL
Can of tomato sauce	7 1/2 oz.	213 mL
Chili powder	2 tsp.	10 mL
Ground cumin	1/4 tsp.	1 mL
Ground allspice	1/8 tsp.	0.5 mL
Can of roasted red peppers, drained and chopped	14 oz.	398 mL

Scramble-fry ground chicken, red onion and jalapeño pepper in olive oil in large frying pan until onion is soft and chicken is no longer pink. Turn into greased 3 quart (3 L) casserole.

Add next 6 ingredients. Stir. Cover. Bake in 350°F (175°C) oven for 1 hour.

Add roasted peppers. Stir. Return to oven. Bake, uncovered, for about 10 minutes until heated through. Makes 9 cups (2.25 L).

1 cup (250 mL): 197 Calories; 8.5 g Total Fat; 676 mg Sodium; 13 g Protein; 18 g Carbohydrate; 2 g Dietary Fiber

Note: Wear gloves when chopping jalapeño peppers and avoid touching your eyes.

 Buy dried herbs and spices in small jars to ensure they're used while the flavor is still at its peak.

Chicken 'N' Chili Pizza

One of the prettiest pizzas you'll ever make.

Boneless, skinless chicken breast half (about 1), slivered	4 oz.	113 g
Cooking oil	1 tsp.	5 mL
Can of red kidney beans, drained and rinsed	14 oz.	398 mL
Small tomato, diced	1	1
Chili powder	2 tsp.	10 mL
Onion powder	1/4 tsp.	1 mL
Garlic powder (optional)	1/8 tsp.	0.5 mL
Partially baked pizza shell (12 inch, 30 cm, size)	1	1
Grated sharp Cheddar cheese	1 1/2 cups	375 mL
Green onions, sliced	2	2
Diced green pepper	1/2 cup	125 mL

Sauté chicken in cooking oil in medium frying pan until no pink remains.

Add next 5 ingredients. Heat for about 5 minutes, stirring and slightly mashing beans, until mixture is fairly dry. Makes 1 3/4 cups (425 mL).

Spread chili over pizza shell. Cover with cheese, green onion and green pepper. Place on greased 12 inch (30 cm) pizza pan. Bake in 425°F (220°C) oven for 10 minutes until crust is brown. Cuts into 8 wedges.

1 wedge: 220 Calories; 8.9 g Total Fat; 343 mg Sodium; 14 g Protein; 21 g Carbohydrate; 3 g Dietary Fiber

Paré Pointer

One little ghost to another: "Here comes my trans-parents."

Meatless Wild Rice Chili

Spicy with a good tomato flavor. The rice adds a nutty flavor.

Chopped onion	1 cup	250 mL
Chopped celery	1 cup	250 mL
Garlic cloves, minced (or 1/2 tsp., 2 mL, powder)	2	2
Olive (or cooking) oil	2 tsp.	10 mL
Vegetable cocktail juice (such as V8), or tomato juice or water	1 cup	250 mL
Water	1 cup	250 mL
Bay leaves	2	2
Wild rice	2/3 cup	150 mL
Can of black beans, rinsed and drained	19 oz.	540 mL
Can of tomato juice	19 oz.	540 mL
Can of white kidney (cannelini) beans, drained and rinsed	19 oz.	540 mL
Can of tomato paste (5 1/2 oz., 156 mL, size)	1/2	1/2
Hot pickled peppers, rinsed and chopped	2 tbsp.	30 mL
Paprika	1 tsp.	5 mL
Ground cumin	1/4 tsp.	1 mL

Sauté onion, celery and garlic in olive oil in large frying pan until soft.

Add cocktail juice and water. Stir. Bring to a boil. Add bay leaves and wild rice. Stir. Cover. Simmer for about 1 hour until rice is tender.

Add remaining 7 ingredients. Stir. Cover. Simmer for about 15 minutes. Remove and discard bay leaves. Makes 8 cups (2 L).

1 cup (250 mL): 185 Calories; 1.9 g Total Fat; 570 mg Sodium; 9 g Protein; 35 g Carbohydrate; 3 g Dietary Fiber

Pictured on front cover.

To have tomato paste on hand for recipes requiring only 1 to 2 tablespoons, drop leftover tomato paste by tablespoons onto greased baking sheet. Freeze for about 1 hour until firm. Wrap individually in waxed paper and store in resealable freezer bag.

Summer Vegetable Chili

All the harvested vegetables of summer combine to make this chili delicious.

Chopped onion	1 1/2 cups	375 mL
Garlic cloves, minced (or 1/2 tsp., 2 mL, powder)	2	2
Cooking oil	1 tbsp.	15 mL
Medium tomatoes, diced (about 4 cups, 1 L)	4	4
Water	3 cups	750 mL
Small zucchini, sliced (about 3 cups, 750 mL)	1	1
Can of chick peas (garbanzo beans), drained and rinsed	19 oz.	540 mL
Fresh green beans, cut into 1 inch (2.5 cm) pieces	1 1/2 cups	375 mL
Fresh (or frozen) kernel corn	1 1/2 cups	375 mL
Chopped celery	1 cup	250 mL
Diced carrot	1 cup	250 mL
Vegetable (or chicken) bouillon powder	3 tbsp.	50 mL
Dried sweet basil	1 tsp.	5 mL
Dried whole oregano	1 tsp.	5 mL
Dried crushed peppers	1/2 tsp.	2 mL
Salt	1/2 tsp.	2 mL
Freshly ground pepper, generous sprinkle		
Jalapeño pepper, seeded and finely diced (see Note)	1	1
Couscous	3/4 cup	175 mL
Fresh cilantro, for garnish		

Sauté onion and garlic in cooking oil in large pot or Dutch oven until onion is soft.

Add next 15 ingredients. Stir. Bring to a boil. Cover. Simmer for 40 minutes until vegetables are tender.

Add couscous. Stir. Cover. Let stand for 10 minutes until liquid is absorbed.

(continued on next page)

Chilies

Sprinkle cilantro over individual servings. Makes 11 1/2 cups (2.9 L).

1 cup (250 mL): 154 Calories; 2.8 g Total Fat; 688 mg Sodium; 6 g Protein; 28 g Carbohydrate; 4 g Dietary Fiber

Pictured on page 72.

Note: Wear gloves when chopping jalapeño peppers and avoid touching your eyes.

Beans Con Queso

Lots of cheese and beans with a slight bite.

Chopped onion	1 cup	250 mL
Garlic clove, minced (or 1/4 tsp., 1 mL, powder)	1	1
Cooking oil	2 tsp.	10 mL
Cans of red kidney beans (14 oz., 398 mL, each), with liquid	2	2
Chopped ripe tomatoes, some seeds removed	2 cups	500 mL
Chili powder	2 tsp.	10 mL
Cayenne pepper	1/8 tsp.	0.5 mL
Grated sharp Cheddar cheese	2 cups	500 mL

Sauté onion and garlic in cooking oil in large frying pan until onion is soft.

Add beans with liquid, tomatoes, chili powder and cayenne pepper. Simmer, uncovered, for about 30 minutes until beans are starting to break up and sauce is thickened.

Add cheese. Heat and stir until melted and combined. Makes 4 cups (1 L).

1 cup (250 mL): 490 Calories; 23.5 g Total Fat; 1130 mg Sodium; 28 g Protein; 44 g Carbohydrate; 2 g Dietary Fiber

Pictured on page 143.

Paré Pointer
He stayed up all night trying to figure out where the sun went and it finally dawned on him.

Chili Potatoes

This recipe uses canned chili for an easy dinner, but
your own homemade chili can be easily substituted.

Olive (or cooking) oil	1 tsp.	5 mL
Medium baking potatoes	2	2
Sea salt (or coarse salt)	2 tsp.	10 mL
Can of chili with beans	14 oz.	398 mL
Salsa	1/2 cup	125 mL
Finely diced green pepper	1/4 cup	60 mL
Finely diced red onion	1/4 cup	60 mL
Grated sharp Cheddar cheese	1/2 cup	125 mL

Cover palms of hands with olive oil. Rub hands over potatoes. Sprinkle
1 tsp. (5 mL) salt all over each potato. Bake directly on center rack in 425°F
(220°C) oven for 45 minutes until tender in center when poked.

Combine chili with beans, salsa, green pepper and red onion in medium
saucepan. Heat until bubbling. Makes 2 2/3 cups (650 mL) chili. Cut
potatoes in half. Fluff inside with a fork. Spoon 1/4 of chili mixture onto
each half. Sprinkle each with 2 tbsp. (30 mL) cheese. Makes 4 stuffed
potato halves.

1 stuffed potato half: 260 Calories; 12.2 g Total Fat; 1933 mg Sodium; 12 g Protein;
29 g Carbohydrate; 6 g Dietary Fiber

1. Cheesy Chili Pasta, page 69
2. Chili And Stuffing, page 60

Props Courtesy Of: Winners Stores

Wheat Berry Chili

Nuttiness of wheat comes through the spiciness. A long cooking time allows the flavors to fully develop.

Unprocessed wheat kernels	1 cup	250 mL
Boiling water	2 cups	500 mL
Can of diced tomatoes, with juice	14 oz.	398 mL
Can of condensed beef bouillon	10 oz.	284 mL
Chili powder	1 tbsp.	15 mL
Garlic clove, minced (or 1/4 tsp., 1 mL, powder)	1	1
Dried crushed chilies	1/2 tsp.	2 mL
Ground cumin	1/2 tsp.	2 mL
Pepper	1/8 tsp.	0.5 mL
Water	2 tbsp.	30 mL
Cornstarch	1 tbsp.	15 mL

Add wheat to boiling water in large saucepan. Reduce heat. Cover. Simmer for 1 hour until wheat pops open.

Add next 7 ingredients. Cover. Simmer for about 1 hour until liquid is reduced.

Stir water into cornstarch in small dish until smooth. Gradually stir into chili. Heat and stir until thickened. Makes 4 cups (1 L).

1 cup (250 mL): 221 Calories; 1.9 g Total Fat; 659 mg Sodium; 9 g Protein; 46 g Carbohydrate; 1 g Dietary Fiber

1. Cheese Twisties, page 141
2. Creamy White Chili, page 80
3. Rich Black Bean Chili, page 58

Props Courtesy Of: The Bay

Veggie Chili With Mixed Beans

All the chopping takes a bit of time unless you use your food processor,
but the result is a nutritious chili that even meat-lovers will like!

Chopped onion	1 cup	250 mL
Cooking oil	2 tbsp.	30 mL
Diced zucchini, with peel	3 cups	750 mL
Coarsely chopped red pepper	1 1/2 cups	375 mL
Coarsely chopped green or yellow pepper	1 1/2 cups	375 mL
Diced parsnip	1 1/2 cups	375 mL
Diced yellow turnip	1 1/2 cups	375 mL
Chopped fresh mushrooms	1 1/2 cups	375 mL
Diced celery	1 cup	250 mL
Diced carrot	1 cup	250 mL
Can of mixed beans, drained and rinsed	19 oz.	540 mL
Can of stewed tomatoes, with juice, broken up	14 oz.	398 mL
Can of tomato paste	5 1/2 oz.	156 mL
Dry white (or alcohol-free) wine	1/2 cup	125 mL
Chili powder	4 tsp.	20 mL
Ground cumin	1 1/2 tsp.	7 mL
Garlic cloves, minced (or 1/2 tsp., 2 mL, powder)	2	2
Salt	1 1/2 tsp.	7 mL
Pepper	1/4 tsp.	1 mL
Grated sharp Cheddar cheese (optional)	1/2 cup	125 mL

Sauté onion in cooking oil in large pot or Dutch oven until soft.

Add next 8 ingredients. Stir. Cover. Cook on medium for about
10 minutes, stirring frequently, until mixture comes to a boil.

Add next 9 ingredients. Stir. Bring to a boil. Reduce heat. Cover. Simmer
for 30 minutes, stirring occasionally, until vegetables are tender.

Sprinkle individual servings with cheese. Makes 12 cups (3 L).

1 cup (250 mL): 127 Calories; 3.2 g Total Fat; 480 mg Sodium; 4 g Protein; 21 g Carbohydrate;
5 g Dietary Fiber

Chilies

Black Bean And Wild Rice Chili

A vegetarian chili that serves as a complete meal or used as a side-dish at your next barbecue. You'll never miss the meat.

Chopped onion	1 1/2 cups	375 mL
Garlic cloves, minced (or 3/4 tsp., 3 mL, powder)	3	3
Olive (or cooking) oil	1 tbsp.	15 mL
Cans of stewed tomatoes (14 oz., 398 mL, each), with juice	2	2
Frozen kernel corn	1/2 cup	125 mL
Diced carrot	1/2 cup	125 mL
Water	1/2 cup	125 mL
Large red pepper, chopped	1	1
Chili powder	2 tsp.	10 mL
Ground allspice	1/2 tsp.	2 mL
Jalapeño pepper, seeded and finely diced (see Note)	1	1
Wild rice	1/2 cup	125 mL
Can of black beans, drained and rinsed	19 oz.	540 mL

Sauté onion and garlic in olive oil in large saucepan or frying pan until onion is soft.

Add next 8 ingredients. Stir. Bring to a boil.

Add wild rice and beans. Stir. Cover. Simmer for 1 1/2 hours, stirring frequently, until rice has split and liquid is mostly absorbed.
Makes 8 cups (2 L).

1 cup (250 mL): 162 Calories; 2.5 g Total Fat; 366 mg Sodium; 7 g Protein; 31 g Carbohydrate; 3 g Dietary Fiber

Note: Wear gloves when chopping jalapeño peppers and avoid touching your eyes.

Bulgur Chili

Healthy grain gives a texture similar to ground beef. Different, but good, flavor.

Garlic cloves, minced (or 3/4 tsp., 3 mL, powder)	3	3
Chopped onion	1 1/2 cups	375 mL
Diced carrot	1 cup	250 mL
Olive (or cooking) oil	1 tbsp.	15 mL
Cans of red kidney beans (14 oz., 398 mL, each), drained and rinsed	2	2
Cans of stewed tomatoes (14 oz., 398 mL, each), with juice, chopped	2	2
Sliced fresh mushrooms	3 cups	750 mL
Chopped green pepper	1 cup	250 mL
Can of tomato sauce	7 1/2 oz.	213 mL
Water	1/2 cup	125 mL
Ground cumin	1 tsp.	5 mL
Chili powder	1 tsp.	5 mL
Dried sweet basil	1 tsp.	5 mL
Bulgur wheat	1 cup	250 mL

Sauté garlic, onion and carrot in olive oil in large frying pan until onion is soft and carrot is tender-crisp. Turn into ungreased 3 quart (3 L) casserole.

Add next 9 ingredients. Stir. Cover. Bake in 350°F (175°C) oven for 1 hour, stirring half-way through cooking time.

Add bulgur. Stir. Cover. Bake for 30 minutes until liquid is mostly absorbed. Makes 10 cups (2.5 L).

1 cup (250 mL): 177 Calories; 2.2 g Total Fat; 474 mg Sodium; 8 g Protein; 35 g Carbohydrate; 7 g Dietary Fiber

Pictured on page 72.

Lentil And Black Bean Chili

Easy to prepare using canned lentils and black beans. Rich, nutty flavor.

Bacon slices	8	8
Chopped onion	1 cup	250 mL
Diced celery	1 cup	250 mL
Diced red or yellow pepper	1 cup	250 mL
Jalapeño pepper, seeded and finely diced (see Note)	1	1
Garlic cloves, minced (or 1/2 tsp., 2 mL, powder)	2	2
Can of cooked green lentils, drained and rinsed	19 oz.	540 mL
Can of black beans, drained and rinsed	19 oz.	540 mL
Can of crushed tomatoes	14 oz.	398 mL
Beer	1 cup	250 mL
Chili powder	2 - 3 tsp.	10 - 15 mL
Ground cumin	1/2 tsp.	2 mL
Ground rosemary	1/8 tsp.	0.5 mL
Lime juice	1 - 2 tsp.	5 - 10 mL

Fry bacon in large frying pan until crisp. Remove with slotted spoon to paper towel. Drain, reserving 2 tbsp. (30 mL) bacon drippings in frying pan. Crumble bacon. Set aside.

Sauté onion, celery, red pepper, jalapeño pepper and garlic in reserved drippings in same frying pan until onion is soft.

Add next 7 ingredients. Stir. Bring to a boil. Reduce heat. Cover. Simmer for 15 minutes to allow flavors to blend.

Add lime juice and bacon. Stir. Makes 7 cups (1.75 L).

1 cup (250 mL): 191 Calories; 4 g Total Fat; 423 mg Sodium; 11 g Protein; 27 g Carbohydrate; 4 g Dietary Fiber

Note: Wear gloves when chopping jalapeño peppers and avoid touching your eyes.

Pork Meatball Chili

Serve with a green salad for a nutritious and tasty meal.

Finely chopped celery	1 cup	250 mL
Finely chopped onion	1 cup	250 mL
Cooking oil	2 tsp.	10 mL
Lean ground pork	1 1/2 lbs.	680 g
Fine dry bread crumbs	3/4 cup	175 mL
Large eggs, fork-beaten	2	2
Seasoned salt	1 tsp.	5 mL
Pepper	1/8 tsp.	0.5 mL
Thinly sliced carrot	3 cups	750 mL
Thinly sliced celery	1 cup	250 mL
Small green pepper, slivered	1	1
Cooking oil	1 tbsp.	15 mL
Can of plum tomatoes, with juice, chopped	28 oz.	796 mL
Chili powder	1 tbsp.	15 mL
Cayenne pepper (optional)	1/8 tsp.	0.5 mL
Cans of white kidney (cannellini) beans (19 oz., 540 mL, each), drained and rinsed	2	2

Sauté celery and onion in first amount of cooking oil in large frying pan until onion is soft. Turn into large bowl.

Add ground pork, bread crumbs, eggs, seasoned salt and pepper to onion mixture. Mix well. Form into 1 inch (2.5 cm) meatballs. Fry meatballs in same frying pan, turning until completely browned. Remove to paper towel. Makes 92 meatballs.

Sauté carrot, celery and green pepper in second amount of cooking oil in same frying pan until carrot is tender-crisp. Turn into large pot or Dutch oven.

Add tomatoes with juice, chili powder, cayenne pepper and beans. Stir. Cover. Simmer for about 10 minutes. Add meatballs. Stir. Cover. Heat for 10 minutes until bubbling and heated through. Makes 14 cups (3.5 L).

1 cup (250 mL): 200 Calories; 6.1 g Total Fat; 394 mg Sodium; 16 g Protein; 21 g Carbohydrate; 2 g Dietary Fiber

Pictured on page 71.

Goulash Chowder

Tomatoes and potatoes in a simple beef broth—with the traditional paprika seasoning, of course!

Chopped onion	1/2 cup	125 mL
Cooking oil	1 tbsp.	15 mL
All-purpose flour	2 tbsp.	30 mL
Boneless inside round (or blade or chuck) steak, trimmed of fat and cubed	3/4 lb.	340 g
Water	4 cups	1 L
Medium potatoes, diced	4	4
Can of diced tomatoes, with juice	14 oz.	398 mL
Frozen kernel corn	1/2 cup	125 mL
Paprika (see Note)	1/2 - 1 tsp.	2 - 5 mL
Granulated sugar	1/2 tsp.	2 mL
Salt	1 tsp.	5 mL
Pepper	1/4 tsp.	1 mL

Sauté onion in cooking oil in large pot or Dutch oven until soft and golden. Stir in flour until well mixed. Turn into small bowl. Set aside.

Put beef and water into same pot. Cover. Simmer for 1 to 1 1/2 hours until tender.

Add next 7 ingredients. Cook for 25 minutes. Add reserved onion mixture. Heat and stir until boiling and thickened. Makes 9 cups (2.25 L).

1 cup (250 mL): 121 Calories; 2.6 g Total Fat; 362 mg Sodium; 11 g Protein; 14 g Carbohydrate; 1 g Dietary Fiber

Note: Hungarian paprika is considered the best flavor but the milder, more common variety was used in testing.

Borscht

You'll like the dill flavor in this borscht.
Not really a chowder, but full of good stuff.

Extra lean ground beef	1 lb.	454 g
Chopped onion	1 cup	250 mL
Cooking oil	1 tsp.	5 mL
Water	5 cups	1.25 L
Baby carrots, sliced	6	6
Can of diced tomatoes, with juice	14 oz.	398 mL
Medium potatoes, diced	2	2
Medium leeks (white and tender parts only), chopped	2	2
Coarsely grated cabbage	1 cup	250 mL
Granulated sugar	1 tsp.	5 mL
Liquid gravy browner	1 tsp.	5 mL
Dill weed	1/2 tsp.	2 mL
Bay leaf	1	1
Cans of beets (14 oz., 398 mL, each), with juice, grated or cut julienne	2	2
Beef bouillon powder	1 1/2 tbsp.	25 mL
Light sour cream	1/2 cup	125 mL
Chopped chives	1 tsp.	5 mL

Scramble-fry ground beef and onion in cooking oil in large uncovered pot or Dutch oven until beef is no longer pink and onion is soft.

Add next 10 ingredients. Stir. Cook for 30 minutes.

Add beets with juice and bouillon powder. Cook for 5 minutes.

Garnish individual servings with dollop of sour cream in center. Sprinkle chives over top. Makes 14 cups (3.5 L).

1 cup (250 mL): 133 Calories; 4.1 g Total Fat; 437 mg Sodium; 8 g Protein; 17 g Carbohydrate; 2 g Dietary Fiber

Pictured on page 126.

Chowders

Quick Corned Beef Chowder

A new use for corned beef. Adds a bit of a nip to this thick soup.

Cans of condensed cream of potato soup (10 oz., 284 mL, each)	2	2
Milk	2 cups	500 mL
Frozen brussels sprouts, thawed and chopped	10 oz.	285 g
Can of corned beef, diced into 1/2 inch (12 mm) cubes	12 oz.	340 g
Frozen peas	1 cup	250 mL
Cayenne pepper	1/4 tsp.	1 mL

Stir soup into milk in large saucepan.

Add brussels sprouts and corned beef. Simmer for about 5 minutes, stirring occasionally, until tender.

Add peas and cayenne pepper. Simmer for 2 to 3 minutes to heat through. Makes 7 1/2 cups (1.9 L).

1 cup (250 mL): 221 Calories; 9.3 g Total Fat; 1158 mg Sodium; 18 g Protein; 16 g Carbohydrate; 2 g Dietary Fiber

Paré Pointer

She thought a drive in restaurant was the place to go if you were trying to curb your appetite.

Kentucky Burgoo

Ber-GOO is a soup filled with a variety of meat and vegetables.
The base is thin but it's a hearty soup nonetheless. Makes a large amount.

Boneless inside round (or blade or chuck) steak, trimmed of fat and cubed	1 lb.	454 g
Water, to cover		
Whole frying chicken, with skin, cut up	3 lbs.	1.4 kg
Boiling water, to cover		
Diced potato	2 1/2 cups	625 mL
Diced carrot	2 cups	500 mL
Chopped onion	1 1/3 cups	325 mL
Diced celery	1 cup	250 mL
Diced yellow turnip	1 cup	250 mL
Coarsely grated cabbage	1 cup	250 mL
Small green pepper, diced	1	1
Can of diced tomatoes, with juice	14 oz.	398 mL
Frozen peas	1 cup	250 mL
Frozen kernel corn	1 cup	250 mL
Parsley flakes	2 tbsp.	30 mL
Worcestershire sauce	2 tsp.	10 mL
Lemon juice	1 tsp.	5 mL
Salt	1 tsp.	5 mL
Cayenne pepper	1/8 tsp.	0.5 mL

Simmer beef in first amount of water in large pot or Dutch oven for 2 hours.

Add chicken. Pour boiling water over all to cover. Cover. Simmer for about 30 minutes until no pink remains in chicken. Remove beef and chicken to cutting board. Reserve liquid. Dice beef. Dice chicken, discarding skin and bones. Skim fat off liquid.

(continued on next page)

100

Return beef and chicken to liquid. Add next 7 ingredients. Cook for about 30 minutes.

Add remaining 8 ingredients. Cook for about 5 minutes. Makes about 18 cups (4.5 L).

1 cup (250 mL): 124 Calories; 1.8 g Total Fat; 241 mg Sodium; 15 g Protein; 12 g Carbohydrate; 2 g Dietary Fiber

Broccoli Chicken Chowder

Generous amounts of chicken in this sage–colored thick soup.
Creamy chicken flavor with the freshness of broccoli.

Packages of frozen cut broccoli (10 oz., 300 g, each), thawed	2	2
Water	1 cup	250 mL
Milk	1 cup	250 mL
Can of skim evaporated milk	13 1/2 oz.	385 mL
Cans of condensed cream of chicken soup (10 oz., 284 mL, each)	2	2
Chicken bouillon powder	1 tbsp.	15 mL
Ground oregano	1/2 tsp.	2 mL
Boneless, skinless chicken breast halves (about 2), diced	1/2 lb.	225 g
Hard margarine (or butter)	1 tbsp.	15 mL

Cook broccoli in water in large saucepan until tender. Do not drain. Purée broccoli with liquid in blender. Return to saucepan.

Add both milks, chicken soup, bouillon powder and oregano. Stir.

Sauté chicken in margarine in frying pan until tender and no pink remains. Add to broccoli mixture. Simmer for about 5 minutes, stirring occasionally. Makes 9 cups (2.25 L).

1 cup (250 mL): 198 Calories; 6.8 g Total Fat; 867 mg Sodium; 20 g Protein; 15 g Carbohydrate; 1 g Dietary Fiber

 For easier removal of fat, and to remove more of it, make broth the day before. Chill liquid overnight and lift off fat in the morning. Reheat remaining broth and meat and proceed with soup recipe.

Mulligatawny

A beautiful yellow-colored soup with a distinctive curry flavor.

Whole frying chicken, skinned and cut up	3 lbs.	1.4 kg
Water	6 cups	1.5 L
Vegetable bouillon powder	2 tbsp.	30 mL
Diced potatoes	2 cups	500 mL
Diced onion	3/4 cup	175 mL
Diced carrot	1/3 cup	75 mL
Diced celery	1/3 cup	75 mL
Diced cooking apple (such as McIntosh)	1 1/3 cups	325 mL
Large tomato, peeled and diced	1	1
Bay leaf	1	1
Garlic powder	1/4 tsp.	1 mL
Curry powder	1/2 - 1 tbsp.	7 - 15 mL
Salt	1 tsp.	5 mL
Pepper	1/4 tsp.	1 mL
Turmeric	1 tsp.	5 mL
Coconut milk	1/2 cup	125 mL
Instant potato flakes	1/4 cup	60 mL
Hot cooked rice	2 cups	500 mL
Lemon slices	8	8

Cook chicken in water and bouillon powder in large pot or Dutch oven for about 30 minutes until tender. Cool enough to handle. Remove chicken. Reserve stock. Discard bones. Set chicken pieces aside.

Add next 12 ingredients to stock. Cook for about 30 minutes until vegetables are tender. Add chicken. Heat through. Remove and discard bay leaf.

Add coconut milk. Stir. Add potato flakes. Heat and stir until boiling and thickened.

Divide rice among 8 individual bowls. Ladle soup over top. Garnish with lemon slices. Makes about 11 cups (2.75 mL).

1 cup (250 mL): 193 Calories; 4.5 g Total Fat; 599 mg Sodium; 16 g Protein; 22 g Carbohydrate; 1 g Dietary Fiber

Chicken Jumble Chowder

Ham, chicken and vegetables retain their flavors in this colorful chowder.

Water	2 1/2 cups	625 mL
Can of diced tomatoes, with juice	14 oz.	398 mL
Diced carrot	1 1/2 cups	375 mL
Chopped green pepper (about 1 small)	1 cup	250 mL
Diced potato	1 cup	250 mL
Chopped onion	3/4 cup	175 mL
Elbow macaroni	1/2 cup	125 mL
Long grain white rice, uncooked	1/3 cup	75 mL
Cans of condensed cream of chicken soup (10 oz., 284 mL, each)	2	2
Milk	2 cups	500 mL
Chopped cooked ham	1 1/2 cups	375 mL
Chopped cooked chicken	1 1/2 cups	375 mL

Combine first 8 ingredients in large pot or Dutch oven. Cover. Cook until carrot is tender, stirring often.

Add remaining 4 ingredients. Mix. Bring to a boil. Reduce heat. Simmer for 5 minutes. Makes 12 cups (3 L).

1 cup (250 mL): 191 Calories; 6.6 g Total Fat; 728 mg Sodium; 13 g Protein; 19 g Carbohydrate; 1 g Dietary Fiber

tip   *For added color and flavor in a soup, toast rice before cooking by frying in a non-stick frying pan on medium, stirring often, until golden.*

Fish Chowder

A thick, white soup that lends itself to whatever seafood you have on hand.
Vegetables add to the appearance. Do not freeze.

Water	2 cups	500 mL
Medium potatoes, peeled and diced	2	2
Medium carrots, diced	2	2
Medium onion, thinly sliced	1	1
Chopped celery	1/4 cup	60 mL
Salt	2 tsp.	10 mL
Pepper	1/4 tsp.	1 mL
Ground thyme	1/4 tsp.	1 mL
Milk	2 1/2 cups	625 mL
Boneless fresh (or frozen) fish fillets, cut into bite-size pieces	14 oz.	400 g
Half-and-half cream	1 cup	250 mL
All-purpose flour	1/4 cup	60 mL

Combine first 8 ingredients in large saucepan. Bring to boil. Reduce heat. Cover. Simmer for about 20 minutes until vegetables are tender.

Add milk and fish. Simmer for 10 minutes.

Stir cream into flour in small bowl until smooth. Gradually stir into fish mixture. Heat and stir until thickened. Makes about 8 cups (2 L).

1 cup (250 mL): 165 Calories; 4.5 g Total Fat; 686 mg Sodium; 14 g Protein; 17 g Carbohydrate; 1 g Dietary Fiber

SEAFOOD CHOWDER SUPREME: Omit fish. Add 5 oz. (142 g) can of each shrimp, crab and clams (or scallops).

It's-A-Cinch Chowder

With only five minutes prep time, this chowder certainly is a "cinch" to make.
And once you've made it, don't let it simmer too long or the fish will toughen.

Finely chopped onion	1/2 cup	125 mL
Hard margarine (or butter)	1 tbsp.	15 mL
Cans of condensed cream of potato soup (10 oz., 284 mL, each)	2	2
Milk	2 cups	500 mL
Boston bluefish (or cod) fillets, half thawed and cut into 3/4 inch (2 cm) cubes	14 oz.	400 g

Parsley, for garnish

Sauté onion in margarine in large pot or Dutch oven until soft and clear. Remove from heat.

Add soup and milk. Stir until blended. Heat and stir until boiling.

Add fish. Bring to a boil. Reduce heat. Simmer for 5 to 8 minutes until fish flakes easily when tested with fork.

Garnish individual servings with parsley. Makes 5 1/2 cups (1.4 L).

1 cup (250 mL): 219 Calories; 8.3 g Total Fat; 989 mg Sodium; 19 g Protein; 16 g Carbohydrate; trace Dietary Fiber

 When making chowders, do not leave the chowder unattended once the milk has been added. Milk comes to a boil very quickly and could easily boil over.

Tuna Chowder

Not the usual chunky chowder, but so thick you don't even need crackers.

Bacon slices, diced	4	4
Milk	3 1/2 cups	875 mL
Can of flaked tuna, drained	6 1/2 oz.	184 g
Skim evaporated milk	1 cup	250 mL
Green onions, thinly sliced	2	2
Onion powder	3/4 tsp.	4 mL
Salt	1/2 tsp.	2 mL
Pepper	1/4 tsp.	1 mL
Celery salt	1/4 tsp.	1 mL
Instant potato flakes	1 cup	250 mL

Fry bacon in large saucepan until cooked but not crisp. Drain.

Add next 8 ingredients. Heat and stir until hot.

Stir in potato flakes, adding more or less until desired consistency. Makes 4 1/2 cups (1.1 L).

1 cup (250 mL): 243 Calories; 5.4 g Total Fat; 719 mg Sodium; 23 g Protein; 26 g Carbohydrate; 1 g Dietary Fiber

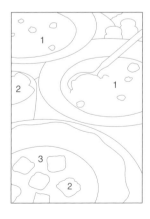

1. Curried Cauliflower Chowder, page 115
2. Croutons, page 146
3. Green Veggie Chowder, page 116

Props Courtesy Of: London Drugs

Speedy Salmon Chowder

*Only five minutes to prepare so keep these ingredients
on hand for a quick dinner.*

Milk	1 cup	250 mL
Can of condensed cream of mushroom soup	10 oz.	284 mL
Can of condensed vegetable soup	10 oz.	284 mL
Can of salmon, drained, skin and round bones removed, broken up	7 1/2 oz.	213 g
Dill weed	1/4 tsp.	1 mL
Onion powder	1/8 tsp.	0.5 mL
Pepper	1/8 tsp.	0.5 mL
Sherry (or alcohol-free sherry)	2 tsp.	10 mL

Whisk milk into mushroom soup in large saucepan until smooth.

Add next 5 ingredients. Heat and stir until bubbling.

Stir in sherry. Makes 4 cups (1 L).

*1 cup (250 mL): 223 Calories; 10.3 g Total Fat; 1383 mg Sodium; 15 g Protein; 16 g Carbohydrate;
1 g Dietary Fiber*

1. Garlic Butter Pull-Aparts, page 135
2. Cheesy Vegetable Chowder, page 114
3. Manhattan Clam Chowder, page 111

Props Courtesy Of: Stokes

Salmon Chowder

The salmon, bacon and potato flavors come through for a
wonderful creamy thick soup.

Bacon slices, diced	4	4
Chopped onion	1 cup	250 mL
Baby carrots, cut into chunks	10	10
Diced celery	1/3 cup	75 mL
Water	1 cup	250 mL
Frozen peas	1/2 cup	125 mL
Cans of condensed cream of potato soup (10 oz., 284 mL, each)	2	2
Can of salmon, drained, skin and round bones removed, broken up	7 1/2 oz.	213 g
Lemon juice	2 tsp.	10 mL
Worcestershire sauce	1 tsp.	5 mL
Salt	1/2 tsp.	2 mL
Pepper	1/8 tsp.	0.5 mL

Sauté bacon and onion in large saucepan until bacon is cooked but not crisp and onion is soft and golden. Drain.

Add carrot, celery and water. Cook for about 15 minutes until vegetables are tender. Do not drain.

Add peas. Cook for about 2 minutes.

Add remaining 6 ingredients. Heat and stir on medium-low until chowder is just starting to simmer. Makes 5 cups (1.25 L).

1 cup (250 mL): 187 Calories; 7.2 g Total Fat; 1518 mg Sodium; 13 g Protein; 17 g Carbohydrate; 1 g Dietary Fiber

Pictured on front cover.

Variation: Use 1/2 lb. (225 g) fresh salmon when in season. Cut into 1 inch (2.5 cm) cubes. Fill saucepan with 1 inch (2.5 cm) water. Cover and bring water to a boil. Add salmon and simmer to poach for about 5 minutes. Drain. Add salmon to chowder.

Manhattan Clam Chowder

This tomato-based traditional chowder is thick with clams
but with a pleasant background of spices. Very satisfying.

Bacon slices, diced	3	3
Finely diced celery	1 cup	250 mL
Finely chopped onion	1 cup	250 mL
Water	3 cups	750 mL
Diced potato	2 cups	500 mL
Can of diced tomatoes, with juice	14 oz.	398 mL
Diced carrot	1 cup	250 mL
Reserved clam juice	1/2 cup	125 mL
Parsley flakes	2 tsp.	10 mL
Salt	3/4 tsp.	4 mL
Ground marjoram	1/2 tsp.	2 mL
Ground thyme	1/4 tsp.	1 mL
Pepper	1/8 tsp.	0.5 mL
Water	2 tbsp.	30 mL
Cornstarch	2 tbsp.	30 mL
Cans of baby clams (5 oz., 142 mL, each), drained and juice reserved	2	2

Sauté bacon, celery and onion in large saucepan until bacon is cooked but not crisp and onion is soft. Drain.

Add next 10 ingredients. Stir. Cover. Cook until boiling and potato and carrot are tender.

Stir water into cornstarch in small cup until smooth. Gradually stir into boiling chowder. Heat and stir until thickened.

Add clams. Stir to heat through. Makes 8 cups (2 L).

1 cup (250 mL): 112 Calories; 1.9 g Total Fat; 428 mg Sodium; 8 g Protein; 16 g Carbohydrate; 2 g Dietary Fiber

Pictured on page 108.

Seafood Bisque

This thick and creamy soup has a very delicate seafood flavor.
A good way to stretch out expensive seafood.

Water	5 cups	1.25 L
Chopped onion	1/2 cup	125 mL
Chopped celery	1/2 cup	125 mL
Medium carrot, chopped	1	1
Chicken bouillon powder	1 1/2 tbsp.	25 mL
Bay leaf	1	1
Hard margarine (or butter), melted	1/4 cup	60 mL
All-purpose flour	1/4 cup	60 mL
Light sour cream	1 cup	250 mL
Can of lobster meat, drained (see Note)	4 oz.	113 g
Can of crabmeat, drained, membrane removed (see Note)	4 oz.	113 g

Combine first 6 ingredients in large pot or Dutch oven. Cover. Cook for about 30 minutes until vegetables are tender.

Stir margarine into flour in medium saucepan until smooth. Gradually stir in about 1/2 of broth from vegetable mixture. Heat and stir until boiling and thickened. Pour back into vegetable mixture. Stir well.

Add remaining 3 ingredients. Remove and discard bay leaf. Process in batches in blender. Return to pot. Heat through without boiling, stirring constantly. Makes 7 cups (1.75 L).

1 cup (250 mL): 165 Calories; 10.3 g Total Fat; 674 mg Sodium; 9 g Protein; 10 g Carbohydrate; 1 g Dietary Fiber

Note: Imitation lobster meat and crabmeat can be used to help keep expenses down.

Chowders

Festive Shrimp Chowder

A combination of shrimp, potato, onion and seasonings. A nice mix.

Chopped onion	1 cup	250 mL
Hard margarine (or butter)	1 tbsp.	15 mL
Water	2 cups	500 mL
Frozen hash brown potatoes	3 cups	750 mL
Milk	3 cups	750 mL
Skim evaporated milk	2/3 cup	150 mL
Chicken bouillon powder	1 tsp.	5 mL
Salt	1/2 tsp.	2 mL
Pepper	1/4 tsp.	1 mL
Ground thyme	1/4 tsp.	1 mL
Frozen cooked shrimp, chopped	1 1/4 lbs.	560 g
Grated light sharp Cheddar cheese	1 cup	250 mL
Instant potato flakes	1/4 cup	60 mL

Sauté onion in margarine in large pot or Dutch oven until soft.

Add water and hash brown potatoes. Cook for about 5 minutes.

Add next 6 ingredients. Stir. Bring to a simmer.

Add shrimp, cheese and potato flakes. Stir gently until heated through and cheese is melted. Makes 9 1/4 cups (2.3 L).

1 cup (250 mL): 240 Calories; 4.8 g Total Fat; 574 mg Sodium; 25 g Protein; 24 g Carbohydrate; 2 g Dietary Fiber

Paré Pointer
He only drives his car in a storm, when it's driving rain.

Cheesy Vegetable Chowder

A tasty pairing of cheese and vegetables.

Chopped onion	1/3 cup	75 mL
Chopped celery	1 tbsp.	15 mL
Hard margarine (or butter)	3 tbsp.	50 mL
All-purpose flour	2 tbsp.	30 mL
Dry mustard	1 tsp.	5 mL
Chicken bouillon powder	2 tsp.	10 mL
Pepper	1/8 tsp.	0.5 mL
Water	2 cups	500 mL
Milk	2 cups	500 mL
Frozen mixed vegetables, cooked	2 cups	500 mL
Pasteurized cheese loaf (such as Velveeta), cut up	1 lb.	500 g
Sherry (or alcohol-free sherry), optional	1/4 cup	60 mL
Grated medium Cheddar cheese, for garnish	1/4 cup	60 mL
Chopped chives, for garnish	2 tbsp.	30 mL

Sauté onion and celery in margarine in large pot or Dutch oven until onion is soft.

Mix in flour, mustard, bouillon powder and pepper.

Add water and milk. Heat and stir until boiling and thickened.

Add vegetables and pasteurized cheese. Stir until heated through and cheese is melted.

Add sherry. Stir.

Garnish individual servings with Cheddar cheese and chives. Makes 6 cups (1.5 L).

1 cup (250 mL): 423 Calories; 30.9 g Total Fat; 1566 mg Sodium; 21 g Protein; 14 g Carbohydrate; trace Dietary Fiber

Pictured on page 108.

Curried Cauliflower Chowder

Plenty of curry flavor but not overpowering.
Very yellow, very chunky and very good.

Chopped onion	1 cup	250 mL
Diced green pepper	1/2 cup	125 mL
Chopped cauliflower	3 cups	750 mL
Water	2 cups	500 mL
Light sour cream	1 cup	250 mL
Milk	1/2 cup	125 mL
Instant potato flakes (or mashed potato)	1/2 cup	125 mL
Chicken bouillon powder	1 tbsp.	15 mL
Curry powder	2 tsp.	10 mL
Salt	1/4 tsp.	1 mL
Pepper	1/8 tsp.	0.5 mL

Cook onion, green pepper and cauliflower in water in large saucepan or Dutch oven until tender. Do not drain.

Add remaining 7 ingredients. Stir. Simmer for 2 to 3 minutes.
Makes 5 cups (1.25 L).

1 cup (250 mL): 108 Calories; 4.3 g Total Fat; 568 mg Sodium; 5 g Protein; 14 g Carbohydrate; 2 g Dietary Fiber

Pictured on page 107.

Variation: Add chopped apricots or dark raisins for a touch of sweetness.

Paré Pointer

The strongest and lightest beams are moon beams
because they hold the moon up.

Green Veggie Chowder

This pretty sage-green chowder is rich only in flavors, not in calories.
A lingering hint of rosemary.

Chopped onion	1 cup	250 mL
Hard margarine (or butter)	1 tbsp.	15 mL
Frozen peas	2 cups	500 mL
Frozen green beans	2 cups	500 mL
Water	2 cups	500 mL
Chicken bouillon powder	1 1/2 tbsp.	25 mL
Ground rosemary	1/4 tsp.	1 mL
Medium potatoes, diced	2	2
Milk	2 cups	500 mL

Bread bowls, page 134
Croutons, page 146, for garnish

Sauté onion in margarine in large pot or Dutch oven until soft.

Add peas, green beans, water, bouillon powder, rosemary and potato. Cover. Cook until potato is tender. Cool slightly. Process in batches in blender. Return to pot.

Add milk. Stir to heat through.

Serve in bread bowls or bowls. Garnish individual servings with croutons. Makes 8 cups (2 L).

1 cup (250 mL): 113 Calories; 2.7 g Total Fat; 461 mg Sodium; 6 g Protein; 17 g Carbohydrate; 2 g Dietary Fiber

Pictured on page 107.

 Fresh herbs make a pretty garnish for soups, stews and chilies. If the supermarket sells them in packages too big for what you need, share with a lucky friend!

Peanut Chowder

*The sweet and tart flavor of the yogurt contrasts well
with the savory peanut flavor.*

Potatoes, cut up	1 lb.	454 g
Sweet potatoes, cut up	1 lb.	454 g
Water	2 cups	500 mL
Cans of condensed chicken broth	2	2
(10 oz., 284 mL, each)		
Can of pumpkin (without spices)	14 oz.	398 mL
Water	1 cup	250 mL
Smooth peanut butter	1/2 cup	125 mL
Salt	1/2 tsp.	2 mL
Pepper	1/4 tsp.	1 mL
Cayenne pepper	1/8 tsp.	0.5 mL
Vanilla yogurt	2/3 cup	150 mL
Chopped chives, for garnish	1/4 cup	60 mL

Place both potatoes in water in large pot or Dutch oven. Cook until tender. Do not drain. Process in batches in blender. Return to pot.

Add next 7 ingredients. Stir. Simmer for about 10 minutes, stirring often.

Swirl individual servings with yogurt. Sprinkle with chives.
Makes 10 cups (2.5 L).

1 cup (250 mL): 208 Calories; 8.2 g Total Fat; 583 mg Sodium; 9 g Protein; 27 g Carbohydrate; 4 g Dietary Fiber

Paré Pointer

*Rather than draw a horse and wagon, he just drew the horse.
He figured the horse could draw the wagon.*

Mushroom And Wild Rice Chowder

An extraordinary mushroom soup! Showy in looks and
rich in flavor. Very different.

Medium onion, halved and sliced	1	1
Medium portabello mushrooms, chopped	2	2
Sliced brown fresh mushrooms	4 cups	1 L
Sliced white fresh mushrooms	4 cups	1 L
Cooking oil	2 tbsp.	30 mL
Water	6 cups	1.5 L
Brown rice	1/4 cup	60 mL
Wild rice	1/4 cup	60 mL
Chicken bouillon powder	2 tbsp.	30 mL
Paprika	1 tsp.	5 mL
Parsley flakes	1 tsp.	5 mL
Salt	1/2 tsp.	2 mL
Water	1/4 cup	60 mL
All-purpose flour	2 tbsp.	30 mL
Cornstarch	1 tbsp.	15 mL
Sour cream	1/2 cup	125 mL
White wine (or alcohol-free), optional	1/2 cup	125 mL

Sauté onion and all mushrooms in 3 or 4 batches in cooking oil in large pot or Dutch oven until lightly browned and liquid is absorbed.

Add next 7 ingredients. Bring to a boil. Cover. Reduce heat. Simmer for about 50 minutes until rice is tender.

Stir water into flour and cornstarch in small cup until smooth. Gradually stir into soup. Heat and stir until boiling and thickened.

Stir in sour cream and wine. Makes 8 cups (2 L).

1 cup (250 mL): 148 Calories; 6.7 g Total Fat; 649 mg Sodium; 5 g Protein; 19 g Carbohydrate; 2 g Dietary Fiber

Minestrone

Love cabbage? Then you'll love this meatless soup.

Finely chopped onion	3/4 cup	175 mL
Medium carrot, grated	1	1
Diced celery	1/2 cup	125 mL
Garlic clove, minced (or 1/4 tsp., 1 mL, powder)	1	1
Olive (or cooking) oil	1 tbsp.	15 mL
Water	6 cups	1.5 L
Can of navy (white) beans, drained and rinsed	19 oz.	540 mL
Coarsely grated cabbage	2 cups	500 mL
Small zucchini, with peel, cut in half lengthwise and sliced (about 2 cups, 500 mL)	1	1
Arborio rice	1/3 cup	75 mL
Chicken bouillon powder	2 tbsp.	30 mL
Ketchup	2 tbsp.	30 mL
Salt	1/2 tsp.	2 mL
Pepper	1/4 tsp.	1 mL
Dried sweet basil	1/4 tsp.	1 mL

Sauté onion, carrot, celery and garlic in olive oil in large pot or Dutch oven until onion is soft.

Add remaining 10 ingredients. Cover. Cook for about 20 minutes. Makes 9 cups (2.25 L).

1 cup (250 mL): 110 Calories; 2.2 g Total Fat; 685 mg Sodium; 4 g Protein; 19 g Carbohydrate; 1 g Dietary Fiber

Potato Chowder

A thick and chunky mix of bacon, potato and pepper.

Bacon slices, diced	6	6
Finely chopped onion	1 cup	250 mL
Thinly sliced celery	1/2 cup	125 mL
Water	2 cups	500 mL
Diced unpeeled new potato	2 cups	500 mL
Seasoned salt	1 tsp.	5 mL
Salt	1/2 tsp.	2 mL
Pepper	1/2 tsp.	2 mL
Bay leaf	1	1
Milk	2 cups	500 mL
Frozen kernel corn	1 cup	250 mL
Milk	1/2 cup	125 mL
All-purpose flour	3 tbsp.	50 mL
Chopped parsley (or chives), for garnish	1 1/2 tbsp.	25 mL

Sauté bacon, onion and celery in medium frying pan until onion is soft. Drain. Set aside.

Combine next 6 ingredients in large saucepan. Cook for about 20 minutes until potato is tender. Remove and discard bay leaf.

Add first amount of milk and corn. Add bacon mixture. Bring to a simmer. Simmer for about 3 minutes until corn is tender.

Stir second amount of milk into flour in small bowl until smooth. Gradually stir into potato mixture. Heat and stir until boiling and thickened.

Sprinkle individual servings with parsley. Makes 6 cups (1.5 L).

1 cup (250 mL): 172 Calories; 4.6 g Total Fat; 565 mg Sodium; 8 g Protein; 26 g Carbohydrate; 2 g Dietary Fiber

Krautfurter Chowder

Sauerkraut fans have to try this. It's not strong, but a mellow blend of flavors.

Medium onion, slivered	1	1
Hard margarine (or butter)	1 tbsp.	15 mL
Sauerkraut, drained and rinsed	2 cups	500 mL
Water	5 cups	1.25 L
Chicken bouillon powder	1 1/2 tbsp.	25 mL
Frozen hash brown potatoes	3 cups	750 mL
Frozen mixed vegetables, cooked	1 1/2 cups	375 mL
European wieners	5	5
Ground rosemary	1/4 tsp.	1 mL
Pepper	1/8 tsp.	0.5 mL

Sauté onion in margarine in large saucepan until soft. Add sauerkraut. Sauté for 3 to 4 minutes.

Add water, bouillon powder, hash brown potatoes and vegetables. Cook on low for about 5 minutes.

Add remaining 3 ingredients. Stir to heat through. Makes 9 2/3 cups (2.4 L).

1 cup (250 mL): 182 Calories; 8.8 g Total Fat; 892 mg Sodium; 6 g Protein; 20 g Carbohydrate; 3 g Dietary Fiber

Pictured on page 125.

 Instead of reaching for the salt, add zip to canned soup with a squirt of lemon or lime or a bit of minced garlic or ginger.

Corn Chowder

Sweet corn flavor stands out from the subtle potato, onion and carrot flavors.
Serve in Bread Bowls, page 134.

Bacon slices, diced	4	4
Chopped onion	1 1/4 cups	300 mL
Diced unpeeled potato	4 cups	1 L
Water	2 cups	500 mL
Grated carrot	1 cup	250 mL
Salt	1 tsp.	5 mL
Chicken bouillon powder	1 tsp.	5 mL
Pepper	1/4 tsp.	1 mL
Celery salt	1/4 tsp.	1 mL
Milk, approximately	2 cups	500 mL
Cans of cream-style corn	2	2
(14 oz., 398 mL, each)		
Chopped parsley, for garnish	2 tbsp.	30 mL

Sauté bacon and onion in large saucepan until onion is soft. Drain.

Add next 7 ingredients. Stir. Cover. Cook until potato and carrot are tender. Do not drain.

Add milk and corn. Stir to heat through.

Garnish individual servings with parsley. Makes 10 cups (2.5 L).

1 cup (250 mL): 163 Calories; 2.3 g Total Fat; 653 mg Sodium; 6 g Protein; 33 g Carbohydrate; 3 g Dietary Fiber

Pictured on page 126.

Paré Pointer
Mom Snake and Dad Snake teach the important
things to Baby Snake: hiss-tory.

Portuguese Chowder

Robust flavor in a rich, red sauce. Serve this hearty soup with bread or buns.

Hot sausage (such as Chorizo or hot Italian)	1/2 lb.	225 g
Chopped onion	1 cup	250 mL
Garlic cloves, minced (or 1/2 tsp., 2 mL, powder)s	2	2
Olive (or cooking) oil	1 tbsp.	15 mL
Can of diced tomatoes, with juice	28 oz.	796 mL
Water	3 cups	750 mL
Diced potato	2 cups	500 mL
Diced celery	1 cup	250 mL
Diced carrot	1 cup	250 mL
Beef bouillon powder	1 tbsp.	15 mL
Finely chopped cabbage	2 cups	500 mL
Diced cooked ham	1 cup	250 mL
Can of kidney beans, with liquid	14 oz.	398 mL
Dry red (or alcohol-free) wine (optional)	1/2 cup	125 mL

Remove sausage meat from casing. Scramble-fry sausage, onion and garlic in olive oil in large pot or Dutch oven until sausage is no longer pink and onion is soft.

Add next 6 ingredients. Bring to a boil. Reduce heat. Simmer for 20 minutes until vegetables are cooked.

Add cabbage, ham and kidney beans. Simmer for 15 minutes until cabbage is tender.

Stir in red wine. Makes 12 cups (3 L).

1 cup (250 mL): 153 Calories; 8.5 g Total Fat; 696 mg Sodium; 8 g Protein; 12 g Carbohydrate; 4 g Dietary Fiber

Lentil Chowder

The individual flavors of all the ingredients are evident in this thick, light-green chowder.

Dried red lentils	1 1/2 cups	375 mL
Water	6 cups	1.5 L
Chopped onion	1 cup	250 mL
Grated carrot	1/2 cup	125 mL
Sliced celery	1/2 cup	125 mL
Diced cooked ham	1 cup	250 mL
Salt (optional)	1/4 tsp.	1 mL
Pepper	1/2 tsp.	2 mL

Combine lentils and water in large pot or Dutch oven. Cover. Cook for 1 hour until tender.

Add onion, carrot and celery. Stir. Cook for 20 minutes.

Add ham, salt and pepper. Stir. Cook for about 10 minutes. Makes 7 cups (1.75 L).

1 cup (250 mL): 193 Calories; 2.3 g Total Fat; 286 mg Sodium; 16 g Protein; 28 g Carbohydrate; 5 g Dietary Fiber

Pictured on page 53.

1. Tomato Herb Bread, page 128
2. Bean Chowder, page 127
3. Krautfurter Chowder, page 121

Props Courtesy Of:
   Alberta Craft Council Craft Gallery Shop
   Soulminder
   Steel And Art Studio

Chowders

Bean Chowder

*If you like brown beans, you'll like this soup. A slight kick
from the cayenne pepper. Good smoky taste.*

Chopped onion	1/2 cup	125 mL
Diced celery	1/2 cup	125 mL
Cooking oil	1 tbsp.	15 mL
Can of beans in tomato sauce	14 oz.	398 mL
Can of condensed tomato soup	10 oz.	284 mL
Milk	1 cup	250 mL
Diced summer sausage	1 cup	250 mL
Water	1/2 cup	125 mL
Grated raw potato	1/2 cup	125 mL
Barbecue sauce	1 tsp.	5 mL
Cayenne pepper	1/8 tsp.	0.5 mL

Sauté onion and celery in cooking oil in large pot or Dutch oven until
onion is soft.

Add remaining 8 ingredients. Stir. Simmer for 15 to 20 minutes until
thickened and potato is tender. Makes 4 1/2 cups (1.1 L).

*1 cup (250 mL): 319 Calories; 15.1 g Total Fat; 1308 mg Sodium; 13 g Protein; 36 g Carbohydrate;
9 g Dietary Fiber*

Pictured on page 125.

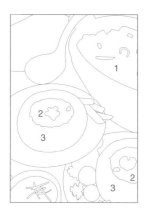

1. Borscht, page 98
2. Corn Chowder, page 122
3. Whole Wheat Bread Bowls, page 134

Tomato Herb Bread

Quick and tasty.

Finely chopped onion	1/2 cup	125 mL
Cooking oil	1 tsp.	5 mL
Granulated sugar	1 tsp.	5 mL
Warm water	1/4 cup	60 mL
Envelope of active dry yeast	1/4 oz.	8 g
(or 2 1/2 tsp., 12 mL, bulk)		
Tomato juice, warmed	1 1/4 cups	300 mL
Olive (or cooking) oil	1 tbsp.	15 mL
Granulated sugar	1 tbsp.	15 mL
Salt	1 tsp.	5 mL
Dried whole oregano	1 tsp.	5 mL
Dried sweet basil	1 tsp.	5 mL
Whole wheat flour	1 1/2 cups	375 mL
Yellow cornmeal	1/4 cup	60 mL
All-purpose flour, approximately	2 cups	500 mL

Sauté onion in cooking oil in small frying pan until clear. Do not brown. Cool. Scrape into large bowl.

Stir sugar into warm water in small bowl until sugar is dissolved. Sprinkle with yeast. Let stand for 10 minutes. Stir to dissolve yeast. Add to onion.

Add next 6 ingredients. Mix.

Add whole wheat flour and cornmeal. Stir. Work in enough all-purpose flour until dough pulls away from sides of bowl. Turn out onto lightly floured surface. Knead for 8 to 10 minutes until smooth and elastic. Put into greased bowl, turning once to grease top. Cover with clean tea towel. Let rise in oven with light on and door closed for about 1 hour until doubled in bulk. Punch dough down. Shape into loaf. Place in greased 9 x 5 x 3 inch (22 x 12.5 x 7.5 cm) loaf pan. Bake in 350°F (175°C) oven for 45 minutes until firm, golden and hollow sounding when tapped. Cuts into 16 slices.

1 slice: 130 Calories; 1.6 g Total Fat; 227 mg Sodium; 4 g Protein; 26 g Carbohydrate; 3 g Dietary Fiber

Pictured on page 125.

Go-Withs

Multigrain Bread

Hearty oval loaf with an even, dense texture but not heavy.
Mild nutty flavor that is delicious with soup, stew or chili.

Whole wheat flour	1 cup	250 mL
Rolled oats (not instant)	1 cup	250 mL
Natural bran	1 cup	250 mL
Yellow cornmeal	1/2 cup	125 mL
Envelope of instant yeast	1/4 oz.	8 g
(or 2 1/2 tsp., 12 mL, bulk)		
Salt	2 tsp.	10 mL
Milk	1 cup	250 mL
Water	1 cup	250 mL
Brown sugar, packed	1/3 cup	75 mL
Olive (or cooking) oil	1/4 cup	60 mL
All-purpose flour, approximately	3 cups	750 mL

Combine first 6 ingredients in large bowl. Make a well in center.

Heat next 4 ingredients in small saucepan until very warm. Pour into well in dry ingredients. Stir until combined.

Add about 2 cups (500 mL) all-purpose flour. Stir. Knead dough, adding more flour as it becomes sticky, for 10 to 15 minutes. Cover with tea towel. Let rest for 15 minutes. Form dough into oval loaves about 8 inches (20 cm) long. Place on large greased baking sheet. Let rise in oven with light on and door closed for 1 hour until doubled in size. Bake in center of 375°F (190°C) oven for 30 minutes until brown and crusty. Makes 2 loaves, 16 slices each.

1 slice: 120 Calories; 2.6 g Total Fat; 154 mg Sodium; 4 g Protein; 22 g Carbohydrate; 2 g Dietary Fiber

Pictured on page 36.

Pine Nut Bread Ring

A very tasty combination of cheese, herbs, garlic and pine nuts. Dough can be divided in half to make two smaller rings, cutting baking time slightly.

Grated part-skim mozzarella cheese	1 cup	250 mL
Cream cheese, softened	4 oz.	125 g
Grated light Parmesan cheese	2 tbsp.	30 mL
Parsley flakes	1 tbsp.	15 mL
Olive (or cooking) oil	2 tsp.	10 mL
Dried sweet basil	1 1/2 tsp.	7 mL
Garlic clove, minced (or 1/4 tsp., 1 mL, powder)	1	1
Freshly ground pepper	1/8 tsp.	0.5 mL
Frozen bread dough (1 lb., 454 g, each), thawed	2	2
Pine nuts, toasted and coarsely chopped	1/3 cup	75 mL

Paprika, sprinkle

Combine first 8 ingredients in small bowl. Set aside. Makes 1 1/3 cups (325 mL) filling.

Knead both loaves of bread together. Roll out on lightly floured surface until large 16 inch (40 cm) square is formed. Spread cream cheese mixture over dough leaving 1/2 inch (12 mm) edge. Sprinkle with pine nuts, reserving 1 tbsp. (15 mL). Roll up, jelly-roll style. Dampen and seal long edge. Place, seam-side down, on greased 11 x 17 inch (28 x 43 cm) baking sheet. Form into ring. Pinch ends together. Make cuts every 1 inch (2.5 cm), from edge to within 1 inch (2.5 cm) of center. Turn each cut section almost on its side so filling is exposed and sections overlap each other.

Sprinkle ring with paprika and reserved pine nuts. Cover. Let rise in oven with light on and door closed for 30 minutes until almost doubled in size. Bake on center rack in 375°F (190°C) oven for 25 to 30 minutes until center of ring is cooked and browned. Makes 1 bread ring. Cuts into 16 slices.

1 slice: 225 Calories; 8.5 g Total Fat; 379 mg Sodium; 8 g Protein; 29 g Carbohydrate; 2 g Dietary Fiber

Pictured on page 35.

Jalapeño Thins

These homemade crisps puff slightly but are not dry or greasy.
Serve with your favorite chili.

All-purpose flour	2 cups	500 mL
Grated Monterey Jack cheese with Jalapeño pepper	1 cup	250 mL
Granulated sugar	1 tbsp.	15 mL
Baking soda	1/2 tsp.	2 mL
Salt	1/2 tsp.	2 mL
Onion powder	1/4 tsp.	1 mL
Cooking oil	1/4 cup	60 mL
Water	1/2 cup	125 mL
Chili powder	1/4 tsp.	1 mL
Ground cumin	1/4 tsp.	1 mL

Combine first 6 ingredients in medium bowl.

Add cooking oil and water. Mix until dough forms a ball. Cover. Let stand for 20 minutes.

Combine chili powder and cumin in small cup. Turn dough out onto lightly floured surface. Divide into 4 portions. Roll 1 portion paper thin into 10 inch (25 cm) circle. Sprinkle with 1/4 of chili powder mixture. Press down lightly. Cut into 8 wedges. Arrange on ungreased baking sheet. Bake in 375°F (190°C) oven for about 12 minutes until crisp and slightly browned. Repeat with remaining dough. Makes 32 wedges.

1 wedge: 62 Calories; 3 g Total Fat; 78 mg Sodium; 2 g Protein; 7 g Carbohydrate; trace Dietary Fiber

Pictured on page 143.

Paré Pointer
She didn't know if she liked raisin bread.
She never tried raisin' any.

Pepper Cheese Bread

This bread goes great with stews or chilies!

Garlic clove, minced	1	1
Mixture of diced green, red, orange and yellow peppers	2/3 cup	150 mL
Green onions, sliced	2	2
Olive (or cooking) oil	2 tsp.	10 mL
Granulated sugar	1 tbsp.	15 mL
Warm water	1/4 cup	60 mL
Envelope of active dry yeast (2 1/2 tsp., 12 mL, bulk)	1/4 oz.	8 g
All-purpose flour	2 cups	500 mL
Warm water	1 1/4 cups	300 mL
Olive (or cooking) oil	1 tbsp.	15 mL
Granulated sugar	1 tbsp.	15 mL
Salt	1 1/4 tsp.	6 mL
All-purpose flour, approximately	1 3/4 cups	425 mL
Grated Monteray Jack with Jalepeño cheese	2/3 cup	150 mL

Sauté garlic, peppers and green onion in first amount of olive oil in small frying pan until soft. Turn into large bowl.

Stir sugar into warm water in small bowl until sugar is dissolved. Sprinkle with yeast. Let stand for 10 minutes. Stir to dissolve yeast. Add to pepper mixture.

Add next 5 ingredients. Stir until smooth mixture is formed.

Work in enough of second amount of flour until dough pulls away from sides of bowl. Turn out onto lightly floured surface. Knead for 8 to 10 minutes, gradually adding cheese, until dough is smooth and elastic. Place in greased bowl, turning once to grease top. Cover with tea towel. Place in oven with light on and door closed for 1 hour until dough is doubled in bulk. Punch dough down. Shape into loaf. Place in 9 x 5 x 3 inch (22 x 12.5 x 7.5 cm) loaf pan. Bake in 350°F (175°C) oven for 40 to 45 minutes until loaf is browned and sounds hollow when tapped on bottom. Turn out onto rack to cool. Cuts into 16 slices.

1 slice: 154 Calories; 3.3 g Total Fat; 213 mg Sodium; 5 g Protein; 26 g Carbohydrate; 1 g Dietary Fiber

Pictured on page 71.

Go-Withs

Quick Pepper Cheese Bread

Frozen bread dough makes this quick. Round loaf with a crisp crust.

Diced green pepper	1/3 cup	75 mL
Diced red pepper	1/3 cup	75 mL
Garlic clove, minced (or 1/4 tsp., 1 mL, powder)	1	1
Green onions, sliced	2	2
Olive (or cooking) oil	2 tsp.	10 mL
Frozen white bread dough, thawed	1 lb.	454 g
Grated pepper Jack cheese	2/3 cup	150 mL

Sauté peppers, garlic and green onion in olive oil in medium frying pan until vegetables are soft. Let cool to room temperature.

Knead bread dough, gradually adding pepper mixture and cheese until well combined. Form dough into 8 inch (20 cm) round. Place on greased baking sheet. Cover with tea towel. Let rise in oven with light on and door closed until doubled in size. Bake on center rack in 350°F (175°C) oven for about 40 minutes until golden. Makes 1 loaf. Cuts into 16 slices.

1 slice: 102 Calories; 3.1 g Total Fat; 180 mg Sodium; 4 g Protein; 15 g Carbohydrate; 1 g Dietary Fiber

Paré Pointer

If you teach a class in knitting, you may be called a knit-wit.

Whole Wheat Bread Bowls

These bowls are edible! Make a "set" for your next Saturday night company.
Perfect for stew, chili or thick chowder.

Granulated sugar	1 tsp.	5 mL
Warm water	1/4 cup	60 mL
Envelope of active dry yeast	1/4 oz.	8 g
(2 1/2 tsp., 12 mL, bulk)		
Whole wheat flour	2 3/4 cups	675 mL
Granulated sugar	3 tbsp.	50 mL
Salt	1 tsp.	5 mL
Hot water	2 1/4 cups	550 mL
Hard margarine (or butter), melted	1 1/2 tbsp.	25 mL
Fancy (mild) molasses	1/4 cup	60 mL
All-purpose flour, approximately	4 cups	1 L

Stir first amount of sugar into warm water in small bowl to dissolve sugar. Sprinkle with yeast. Let stand for 10 minutes. Stir to dissolve yeast.

Combine whole wheat flour, second amount of sugar and salt in large bowl. Add yeast mixture. Stir.

Combine hot water, margarine and molasses in medium bowl. Add to dough. Stir.

Work in enough remaining flour until dough pulls away from sides of bowl. Turn out onto lightly floured surface. Knead for 8 to 10 minutes until smooth and elastic. Place in greased bowl, turning once to grease top. Cover with clean tea towel. Let stand in oven with light on and door closed for 45 to 60 minutes until doubled in bulk. Punch down dough. Divide into 8 equal portions. Shape into round balls. Place on greased baking sheet well apart from each other. Grease surface of dough. Cover with tea towel. Let rise in oven with light on and door closed for about 1 hour until doubled in size. Bake in 375°F (190°C) oven for 20 minutes. Cool. Slice off top of loaf. Remove inside of loaf, leaving 1/2 inch (12 mm) shell, forming bowl. Makes 8 bread bowls, each large enough to hold about 1 to 1 1/2 cups (250 to 375 mL) soup.

1 bread bowl: 462 Calories; 3.9 g Total Fat; 333 mg Sodium; 13 g Protein; 95 g Carbohydrate; 8 g Dietary Fiber

Pictured on page 126.

Garlic Butter Pull-Aparts

These buns not only taste great, they are also fun to eat.

Frozen white bread dough, thawed	1 lb.	454 g
Hard margarine (or butter), melted	1/4 cup	60 mL
Parsley flakes	2 tsp.	10 mL
Garlic cloves, minced (or 1/2 tsp., 2 mL, powder)	2	2

Cut dough into 16 pieces. Loosely drop 8 pieces into center of 9 x 5 x 3 inch (22 x 12.5 x 7.5 cm) loaf pan.

Combine margarine, parsley flakes and garlic in small bowl. Drizzle 1/2 of margarine mixture all over dough pieces in pan. Lay remaining bread dough pieces over top. Drizzle remaining margarine mixture over top. Cover loosely with greased waxed paper. Let rise in oven with light on and door closed for about 40 minutes until doubled in size. Bake in 350°F (175°C) oven for about 30 minutes until golden. Cool for about 30 minutes before turning loaf out onto rack. Serves 16.

1 serving: 104 Calories; 4.1 g Total Fat; 189 mg Sodium; 2 g Protein; 14 g Carbohydrate; 1 g Dietary Fiber

Pictured on page 108.

 Save removed bread for dipping in soup or gravy or cut into 3/4 inch (2 cm) pieces and dry in warm oven to use as croutons.

Rich Tea Biscuits

Always a last minute favorite. So speedy to make.
Be sure to try all the variations. Previously published in
Company's Coming Muffins & More, page 94.

All-purpose flour	2 cups	500 mL
Granulated sugar	2 tbsp.	30 mL
Baking powder	4 tsp.	20 mL
Salt	1 tsp.	5 mL
Cream of tartar	1/2 tsp.	2 mL
Hard margarine (or butter), cold	1/2 cup	125 mL
Cold milk	3/4 cup	175 mL

Combine first 5 ingredients in medium bowl. Stir thoroughly.

Cut in margarine until crumbly. Pour in milk. Stir quickly to combine. Dough should be soft. Turn out onto lightly floured surface. Knead gently 8 to 10 times. Roll or pat 1/2 to 3/4 inch (1.2 to 2 cm) thick or half the thickness you want the baked product to be. Cut with 2 inch (5 cm) cookie cutter. Place on greased baking sheet, close together for soft sides or apart for crisp sides. Bake in 450°F (230°C) oven for 12 to 15 minutes. Brushing biscuits with milk before baking will produce a pretty brown top. Makes 12 to 16 biscuits.

1 biscuit: 201 Calories; 10.2 g Total Fat; 495 mg Sodium; 3 g Protein; 24 g Carbohydrate; 1 g Dietary Fiber

BISCUIT TOPPING: Place biscuits close together on hot casserole. Bake in 425°F (220°C) oven for 20 to 25 minutes. If casserole won't hold all of them, bake on separate baking sheet.

BUTTERMILK BISCUITS: Reduce baking powder to 2 tsp. (10 mL). Add 1/2 tsp. (2 mL) baking soda. Replace milk with buttermilk.

COCONUT ROLLS: Spread rolled rectangle of dough with mixture of 1/3 cup (75 mL) brown sugar, packed and 1/3 cup (75 mL) medium coconut. Roll and cut into 12 slices. Bake as for Rich Tea Biscuits.

GRAHAM BISCUITS: Use 1/2 cup (125 mL) hard margarine (or butter). Reduce flour to 1 1/2 cups (375 mL). Add 1 cup (250 mL) graham cracker crumbs. A distinctive flavor.

(continued on next page)

ORANGE BISCUITS: Add 1 tbsp. (15 mL) grated orange rind. Substitute half orange juice for half of milk. Dip sugar cubes in some orange juice and press in top of each biscuit before baking.

PEANUT BUTTER BISCUITS: Reduce margarine to 1/4 cup (60 mL). Add 1/4 cup (60 mL) peanut butter.

PIZZA CRUST: Make dough as above. Press or roll to size of pizza pan. Proceed to make your favorite pizza.

TOMATO BISCUITS: Omit milk. Add 3/4 cup (175 mL) tomato juice. Add 1/2 cup (125 mL) grated cheese (optional).

Parmesan Bread

A tasty bread for those who don't like having garlic breath after a meal.

Hard margarine (or butter), softened	6 tbsp.	100 mL
Grated Parmesan cheese	1/4 cup	60 mL
Crushed dried sweet basil	1/4 tsp.	1 mL
French bread loaf, cut into 1 inch (2.5 cm) slices	1	1

Combine margarine, Parmesan cheese and basil in small bowl.

Spread both sides of each bread slice lightly with margarine mixture. Reshape into loaf. Wrap in foil. Bake in 350°F (175°C) oven for 20 minutes. Cuts into 12 to 14 slices.

1 slice: 166 Calories: 7.6 g Total Fat; 340 mg Sodium; 4 g Protein; 20 Carbohydrate; 1 g Dietary Fiber

 To test your baking powder to see if it's active, pour 1/4 cup (60 mL) of hot water over 1/2 tsp. (2 mL) of baking powder. It should bubble. If there is a weak reaction, or none at all, you need to run to the store for a new container.

Bread Twists

Little effort and lots of eye—and taste—appeal.

All-purpose flour	2 cups	500 mL
Oat bran	1/4 cup	60 mL
Envelope of instant yeast	1/4 oz.	8 g
(2 1/2 tsp., 12 mL, bulk)		
Large eggs, fork-beaten	2	2
Cooking oil	2 tbsp.	30 mL
Fancy (mild) molasses	3 tbsp.	50 mL
Very warm water	1 1/2 cups	375 mL
Salt	1/2 tsp.	2 mL
Whole wheat flour, approximately	2 1/2 cups	625 mL
Seven grain mix	1/4 cup	60 mL
Sesame seeds	1/4 cup	60 mL
Yellow cornmeal	1/4 cup	60 mL
Egg white (large)	1	1
Water	1 tbsp.	15 mL

Combine all-purpose flour, bran and yeast in large bowl.

Combine eggs, cooking oil, molasses, water and salt in small bowl. Add to flour mixture. Mix well.

Work in enough whole wheat flour until dough pulls away from sides of bowl. Cover with tea towel. Let stand in oven with light on and door closed for 20 minutes. Punch dough down. Shape into twists by splitting dough into 18 equal pieces. Roll each piece into 14 inch (35 cm) rope. Fold rope in half. Twist each rope about 4 or 5 times.

Place grain mix, sesame seeds and cornmeal in separate bowls.

Beat egg white and water with fork in small cup. Brush surface of twists, top and bottom. Roll in topping of your choice. Arrange on greased baking sheet. Cover with tea towel. Let stand in oven with light on and door closed for about 30 minutes until doubled in size. Bake in 350°F (175°C) oven for 20 minutes. Makes 18 twists.

1 twist: 177 Calories; 3.9 g Total Fat; 79 mg Sodium; 6 g Protein; 31 g Carbohydrate; 3 g Dietary Fiber

Pictured on front cover.

Go-Withs

Quick Bread Sticks

The let's-eat-now breadsticks.

Package of refrigerated country-style biscuits (10 biscuits per tube)	1	1
Egg white (large), fork-beaten	1	1
Seasoned salt (optional)		
Italian seasoning (optional)		
Sesame seeds (optional)		

Roll each biscuit into ropes about 10 inches (25 cm) long. Place about 1 inch (2.5 cm) apart on greased baking sheet.

Brush tops with egg whites.

Sprinkle with toppings of your choice. Bake in 450°F (230°C) oven for 10 minutes. Makes 10 bread sticks.

1 bread stick: 61 Calories; 1 g Total Fat; 292 mg Sodium; 2 g Protein; 11 g Carbohydrate; 0 g Dietary Fiber

Variation: Brush with margarine. Sprinkle with your choice of salt, onion salt, garlic salt, oregano, basil.

Paré Pointer

A piano teacher's dog is one whose Bach is worse than his bite.

Dipping Sticks

These soft breadsticks are versatile go-withs for stews, chilies and chowders.

Whole wheat flour	1 cup	250 mL
Active dry yeast	2 tsp.	10 mL
Salt	1 tsp.	5 mL
Hot water	2/3 cup	150 mL
Cooking oil	2 tbsp.	30 mL
Liquid honey	1 tbsp.	15 mL
All-purpose flour, approximately	1 1/4 cups	300 mL
Egg white (large), fork-beaten	1	1
Water	1 tsp.	5 mL
Sesame seeds, sprinkle		
Poppy seeds, sprinkle		
Caraway seeds, sprinkle		
Coarse sea salt, sprinkle		

Combine whole wheat flour, yeast and salt in large bowl.

Combine hot water, cooking oil and honey in small bowl. Add to flour mixture. Beat for about 3 minutes.

Stir in enough all-purpose flour until soft dough is formed. Turn out onto lightly floured surface. Knead until stiff dough is formed. Cover with tea towel. Let rest for 30 minutes. Divide dough into 4 equal portions. Divide each portion into 4 equal pieces. Let dough rest for 20 minutes. Roll each piece between palms of hands on lightly floured surface into 10 inch (25 cm) bread stick. Place 1 inch (2.5 cm) apart on greased baking sheets.

Combine egg white and water in small cup. Brush over top of bread sticks. Sprinkle with your choice of toppings. Bake in 325°F (160°C) oven for 20 minutes until crisp and golden. Makes 16 sticks.

1 stick: 79 Calories; 1.9 g Total Fat; 153 mg Sodium; 2 g Protein; 13 g Carbohydrate; 1 g Dietary Fiber

Pictured on page 53.

Cheese Twisties

A wonderful Italian flavor. Would go nice with Rich Seafood Stew, page 40.

Frozen bread dough, thawed	1 lb.	454 g
Sun-dried tomato pesto (or basil)	1/4 cup	60 mL
Grated part-skim mozzarella cheese	3/4 cup	175 mL
Large egg, fork-beaten	1	1
Water	1 tbsp.	15 mL
Sesame seeds	2 tsp.	10 mL
Flax seeds	2 tsp.	10 mL

Roll out dough on lightly floured surface to 12 x 12 inch (30 x 30 cm) rectangle. Spread with pesto. Sprinkle with cheese. Press down lightly. Fold into thirds until 4 x 12 inch (10 x 30 cm) rectangle is formed. Cut crosswise with sharp knife into 1/2 inch (12 mm) strips. Twist each strip once or twice. Arrange on greased baking sheet 2 inches (5 cm) apart. Cover. Let rise in oven with light on and door closed for 40 minutes until almost doubled in size.

Combine egg and water in small cup. Brush over twists.

Combine sesame and flax seeds in small cup. Sprinkle lightly over twists. Bake on center rack in 375°F (190°C) oven for 13 to 15 minutes until golden. Makes 24 twisties.

1 twistie: 70 Calories; 2.1 g Total Fat; 122 mg Sodium; 3 g Protein; 10 g Carbohydrate; trace Dietary Fiber

Pictured on page 90.

 Keep portions of cheese in the freezer for easier grating. Grating cheese at fridge or room temperature is more difficult.

Pumpkin Corn Cakes

Serve these moist, dense muffins with Creamy White Chili, page 80.

Yellow cornmeal	2 1/2 cups	625 mL
1% buttermilk	1 2/3 cups	400 mL
Can of pumpkin (without spices)	14 oz.	398 mL
Hard margarine (or butter), melted	1/3 cup	75 mL
Maple-flavored syrup	1/3 cup	75 mL
Large eggs, fork-beaten	2	2
All-purpose flour	1 2/3 cups	400 mL
Baking powder	1 tbsp.	15 mL
Baking soda	3/4 tsp.	4 mL
Salt	1/2 tsp.	2 mL
Ground cardamom	1/2 tsp.	2 mL

Combine first 6 ingredients in large bowl.

Combine flour, baking powder, baking soda, salt and cardamom in medium bowl. Add to cornmeal mixture. Stir until just moistened. Place 1/3 cup (75 mL) batter into each of 24 greased muffin cups. Bake in 375°F (190°C) oven for 20 minutes. Makes 24 corn cakes.

1 muffin: 145 Calories; 3.6 g Total Fat; 198 mg Sodium; 4 g Protein; 25 g Carbohydrate; 1 g Dietary Fiber

Pictured on page 17.

Variation: Omit muffin cups. Place batter in 2 greased 8 × 8 inch (20 × 20 cm) round cake pans. Bake in 350°F (175°C) oven for about 30 minutes. Makes 2 cakes.

1. Jalapeño Thins, page 131
2. Beans Con Queso, page 87

Props Courtesy Of: Treasure Barrel

Go-Withs

Individual Focaccia

*Now you don't have to share! Serve a basket of all
the variations with your next pot of chili.*

Frozen yeast dough buns, thawed	8	8
Sun-dried tomato pesto	3 tbsp.	50 mL
Chopped ripe olives	3 tbsp.	50 mL
Sea salt (optional)	1 tbsp.	15 mL

Place dough portions on greased baking sheet. Cover with tea towel. Let
stand in oven with light on and door closed for about 30 minutes.

Roll out each portion into 4 1/2 inch (11 cm) circle. Arrange on greased
baking sheets. Spread with 1 tsp. (5 mL) pesto. Sprinkle with olives. Press
olives lightly into bread making dents. Sprinkle with salt. Cover with waxed
paper and tea towel. Let rise in oven with light on and door closed for
20 to 30 minutes until puffy. Bake on center rack in 425°F (220°C) oven for
about 8 minutes until golden. Makes 8 focaccia.

*1 focaccia: 93 Calories; 2.7 g Total Fat; 174 mg Sodium; 3 g Protein; 15 g Carbohydrate;
1 g Dietary Fiber*

Pictured on page 144 and back cover.

Variation: Omit sun-dried tomato pesto and olives. Use basil tomato pesto
and finely chopped red onion.

Variation: Brush with olive oil. Divide and sprinkle 3 tbsp. (50 mL) Romano
cheese and 1 tbsp. (15 mL) dill weed on each bread top before baking.

Variation: Brush with 2 tbsp. (30 mL) olive oil. Sprinkle with 2 tbsp.
(30 mL) Italian seasoning.

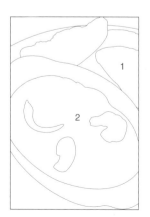

1. Individual Focaccia, page 145
2. Easy Cioppino, page 41

Props Courtesy Of: The Bay

Croutons

Great garlic flavor for soup or salad.

Hard margarine (or butter), softened	1/4 cup	60 mL
Grated Parmesan cheese	2 tsp.	10 mL
Garlic clove, minced (or 1/4 tsp., 1 mL, powder)	1	1
Slices of day-old whole wheat (or white) sandwich bread	6	6

Combine first 3 ingredients in small bowl.

Spread a light coating of margarine mixture on both sides of bread slices. Cut each slice into 25 cubes. Place on baking sheet. Broil in center of oven for about 4 minutes, stirring cubes several times, until golden brown. Makes 150 croutons or 4 cups (1 L).

1/4 cup (60 mL): 55 Calories; 3.6 g Total Fat; 97 mg Sodium; 1 g Protein; 5 g Carbohydrate; 1 g Dietary Fiber

Pictured on page 107.

Variation: Omit Parmesan cheese. Add 1/2 tsp. (2 mL) Italian seasoning. Stir.

Piccalilli

A very tasty use for green tomatoes. Previously published in Company's Coming Preserves, page 70.

Green tomatoes (about 9 cups, 2.25 L), stem ends and cores removed, chopped	3 lbs.	1.4 kg
Chopped onion	4 cups	1 L
Small green pepper, chopped	1	1
Coarse (pickling) salt	1/2 cup	125 mL
White vinegar	3 cups	750 mL
Granulated sugar	3 cups	750 mL
Mixed pickling spice, tied in double layer of cheesecloth	1 tbsp.	15 mL
Mustard seed	1 tsp.	5 mL

(continued on next page)

Go-Withs

Mix first 4 ingredients in large bowl. Cover. Let stand on counter overnight. Drain well, pressing to remove juice.

Combine vinegar, sugar, pickling spice and mustard seed in large pot or Dutch oven. Add drained vegetables. Bring to a boil, stirring frequently. Reduce heat. Simmer, uncovered, for about 5 minutes until vegetables are half done. Discard spice bag. Pour into hot sterilized pint (2 cup, 500 mL) jars to within 1/2 inch (12 mm) of top. Place sterilized metal lids on jars and screw metal bands on securely. Process in a boiling water bath for 5 minutes. Makes 10 cups (2.5 L), enough for 5 pint jars.

1/2 cup (125 mL): 140 Calories; 0.2 g Total Fat; 1250 mg Sodium; 1 g Protein; 35 g Carbohydrate; 1 g Dietary Fiber

Sliced Pickled Peppers

Use a crinkle cutter to make fancy slices. Color will change and fade slightly.

Whole red and yellow hot peppers (habanero or jalepeño), see Note	3 cups	750 mL
White vinegar	1 cup	250 mL
Granulated sugar	1/2 cup	125 mL
Coarse (pickling) salt	4 tsp.	20 mL
Olive oil	1/4 cup	60 mL

Slice off stem end of peppers. Scrape out and discard seeds and ribs from peppers. Slice peppers crosswise, making rings. Pack into hot sterilized pint (2 cup, 500 mL) jar.

Heat vinegar, sugar, coarse salt and olive oil in stainless steel or other non-reactive saucepan until sugar and salt are dissolved. Do not boil. Pour hot brine over peppers to within 1/2 inch (12 mm) of top. Place sterilized metal lid on jar and screw metal band on securely. Cool. Store in refrigerator for 2 days before serving. Stores for up to 1 month. Makes 2 cups (500 mL), enough for 1 pint jar.

1/4 cup (60 mL) pickled peppers: 126 Calories; 6.5 g Total Fat; 1053 mg Sodium; 1 g Protein; 18 g Carbohydrate; 1 g Dietary Fiber

Pictured on page 72.

Note: Wear gloves when chopping hot peppers and avoid touching your eyes.

Cool Cukes

A great pickle that you can make one day and serve the next. Previously published in Company's Coming Vegetables, page 102.

Granulated sugar	2 cups	500 mL
White vinegar	1 cup	250 mL
Coarse (pickling) salt	1/4 cup	60 mL
Mustard seed	1 tsp.	5 mL
Celery seed	1 tsp.	5 mL
Thinly sliced English cucumber, with peel	8 cups	2 L
Sliced onion	1 cup	250 mL
Medium red peppers, slivered	2	2
Medium green peppers, slivered	2	2

Combine first 5 ingredients in large container. Don't worry about dissolving salt. It will dissolve on its own.

Put cucumber, onion and peppers into separate large container. Pour vinegar mixture over top. Chill overnight before serving. Will keep for ages in refrigerator. Makes about 8 cups (2 L).

1/2 cup (125 mL) pickled cucumber: 112 Calories; 0.2 g Total Fat; 1553 mg Sodium; 1 g Protein; 28 g Carbohydrate; 1 g Dietary Fiber

Hot Pickled Peppers

This recipe can easily be doubled or tripled.

Whole large hot peppers (habanero or jalapeño), variety of colors (see Note)	7 - 8	7 - 8
White vinegar	3 cups	750 mL
Granulated sugar	1 cup	250 mL
Coarse (pickling) salt	1 tbsp.	15 mL

Wash peppers well, particularly around stem. Trim stems to 1/4 inch (6 mm). Make 3 or 4 slits in each of the peppers. Pack firmly into hot sterilized 1 quart (1 L) jars. Do not squish.

(continued on next page)

148

Go-Withs

Heat vinegar, sugar and coarse salt in stainless steel or other non-reactive saucepan until sugar and salt are dissolved. Do not boil. Pour over peppers to within 1/2 inch (12 mm) of top. Place sterilized metal lid on jar and screw metal band on securely. Process in a boiling water bath for 10 minutes. Cool. Store for 3 to 4 weeks before using. Makes 1 quart (1 L).

1 large pickled pepper: 83 Calories; 0.1 g Total Fat; 509 mg Sodium; 1 g Protein; 22 g Carbohydrate; 1 g Dietary Fiber

Pictured on page 17.

Note: For amount of brine above:
　　Large peppers—7 to 8 = 1 quart jar
　　Medium peppers—21 = 1 quart jar
　　Small peppers—4 cups (1 L) = 4 half pint jars = 2 pint jars = 1 quart jar

---

Dilled Cukes

Crispy and tangy, these pickles will give you a taste of summer all year.

English cucumber, with peel, scored with fork tines	1	1
Water	2 2/3 cup	650 mL
White vinegar	1/2 cup	125 mL
Salt	1 tbsp.	15 mL
Granulated sugar	1 tbsp.	15 mL
Dill weed	1 tsp.	5 mL
Garlic powder	1/2 tsp.	2 mL

Cut cucumber lengthwise into spears about 4 inches (10 cm) long. Place upright in container.

Combine remaining 6 ingredients in small saucepan. Bring to a boil, stirring often. Pour over cucumber. Cover. Chill for 1 or 2 days. Makes 24 slices.

1 pickled slice: 5 Calories; trace Total Fat; 295 mg Sodium; trace Protein; 1 g Carbohydrate; trace Dietary Fiber

Speedy Beet Pickles

Definitely no work to these. Canned beets are marinated for a day or two and then are ready to eat. Try both kinds to determine your preference. Previously published in Company's Coming Preserves, page 100.

Cans of beets (14 oz. 398 mL, each), drained and juice reserved (see Note)	2	2
Reserved beet juice	1 cup	250 mL
White vinegar	1 cup	250 mL
Granulated sugar	1/2 cup	125 mL
Table salt	1/2 tsp.	2 mL

Cut larger beets. Leave tiny ones whole. Place in quart jar.

Combine beet juice, vinegar, sugar and salt in container. Stir until sugar dissolves. Pour over beets. Cover. Chill for 1 or 2 days before serving. Keeps in refrigerator for at least 4 weeks. Makes 4 cups (1 L), enough for 1 quart jar.

4 cups (1 L) pickled beets: 679 Calories; 0.1 g Total Fat; 3367 mg Sodium; 7 g Protein; 174 g Carbohydrate; 9 g Dietary Fiber

Note: Fresh cooked beets (about 3 1/2 cups, 875 mL) may be used instead of canned, reserving 1 cup (250 mL) cooking liquid.

SPICED PICKLED BEETS: Add 1/2 cup (125 mL) sugar and 1 tbsp. (15 mL) mixed pickling spice that you have tied in a double layer of cheesecloth. Boil on medium for 5 minutes. Discard spice bag. Pour brine over beets. Chill for 1 or 2 days before serving. Keeps in refrigerator for at least 4 weeks.

Paré Pointer
An educated hole in the wall is better known as a wise crack.

Go-Withs

Measurement Tables

Throughout this book measurements are given in Conventional and Metric measure. To compensate for differences between the two measurements due to rounding, a full metric measure is not always used. The cup used is the standard 8 fluid ounce. Temperature is given in degrees Fahrenheit and Celsius. Baking pan measurements are in inches and centimetres as well as quarts and litres. An exact metric conversion is given below as well as the working equivalent (Metric Standard Measure).

Spoons

Conventional Measure	Metric Exact Conversion Millilitre (mL)	Metric Standard Measure Millilitre (mL)
1/8 teaspoon (tsp.)	0.6 mL	0.5 mL
1/4 teaspoon (tsp.)	1.2 mL	1 mL
1/2 teaspoon (tsp.)	2.4 mL	2 mL
1 teaspoon (tsp.)	4.7 mL	5 mL
2 teaspoons (tsp.)	9.4 mL	10 mL
1 tablespoon (tbsp.)	14.2 mL	15 mL

Cups

Conventional Measure	Metric Exact Conversion Millilitre (mL)	Metric Standard Measure Millilitre (mL)
1/4 cup (4 tbsp.)	56.8 mL	60 mL
1/3 cup (5 1/3 tbsp.)	75.6 mL	75 mL
1/2 cup (8 tbsp.)	113.7 mL	125 mL
2/3 cup (10 2/3 tbsp.)	151.2 mL	150 mL
3/4 cup (12 tbsp.)	170.5 mL	175 mL
1 cup (16 tbsp.)	227.3 mL	250 mL
4 1/2 cups	1022.9 mL	1000 mL (1 L)

Oven Temperatures

Fahrenheit (°F)	Celsius (°C)
175°	80°
200°	95°
225°	110°
250°	120°
275°	140°
300°	150°
325°	160°
350°	175°
375°	190°
400°	205°
425°	220°
450°	230°
475°	240°
500°	260°

Dry Measurements

Conventional Measure Ounces (oz.)	Metric Exact Conversion Grams (g)	Metric Standard Measure Grams (g)
1 oz.	28.3 g	28 g
2 oz.	56.7 g	57 g
3 oz.	85.0 g	85 g
4 oz.	113.4 g	125 g
5 oz.	141.7 g	140 g
6 oz.	170.1 g	170 g
7 oz.	198.4 g	200 g
8 oz.	226.8 g	250 g
16 oz.	453.6 g	500 g
32 oz.	907.2 g	1000 g (1 kg)

Pans

Conventional Inches	Metric Centimetres
8x8 inch	20x20 cm
9x9 inch	22x22 cm
9x13 inch	22x33 cm
10x15 inch	25x38 cm
11x17 inch	28x43 cm
8x2 inch round	20x5 cm
9x2 inch round	22x5 cm
10x4 1/2 inch tube	25x11 cm
8x4x3 inch loaf	20x10x7.5 cm
9x5x3 inch loaf	22x12.5x7.5 cm

Casseroles

CANADA & BRITAIN Standard Size Casserole	Exact Metric Measure	UNITED STATES Standard Size Casserole	Exact Metric Measure
1 qt. (5 cups)	1.13 L	1 qt. (4 cups)	900 mL
1 1/2 qts. (7 1/2 cups)	1.69 L	1 1/2 qts. (6 cups)	1.35 L
2 qts. (10 cups)	2.25 L	2 qts. (8 cups)	1.8 L
2 1/2 qts. (12 1/2 cups)	2.81 L	2 1/2 qts. (10 cups)	2.25 L
3 qts. (15 cups)	3.38 L	3 qts. (12 cups)	2.7 L
4 qts. (20 cups)	4.5 L	4 qts. (16 cups)	3.6 L
5 qts. (25 cups)	5.63 L	5 qts. (20 cups)	4.5 L

Photo Index

Tip Index

Recipe Index

155

156

Company's Coming cookbooks are available at retail locations throughout Canada!

EXCLUSIVE mail order offer on next page

Buy any 2 cookbooks—choose a 3rd FREE of equal or lesser value than the lowest price paid.

Original Series — CA$15.99 Canada — US$12.99 USA & International

CODE		CODE		CODE	
SQ	150 Delicious Squares	PB	The Potato Book	SDPP	School Days Party Pack
CA	Casseroles	CCLFC	Low-Fat Cooking	HS	Herbs & Spices
MU	Muffins & More	CFK	Cook For Kids	BEV	The Beverage Book
SA	Salads	SCH	Stews, Chilies & Chowders	SCD	Slow Cooker Dinners
AP	Appetizers	FD	Fondues	WM	30-Minute Weekday Meals
SS	Soups & Sandwiches	CCBE	The Beef Book	SDL	School Days Lunches
CO	Cookies	RC	The Rookie Cook	PD	Potluck Dishes
PA	Pasta	RHR	Rush-Hour Recipes	GBR	Ground Beef Recipes
BA	Barbecues	SW	Sweet Cravings	FRIR	4-Ingredient Recipes
PR	Preserves	YRG	Year-Round Grilling	KHC	Kids' Healthy Cooking
CH	Chicken, Etc.	GG	Garden Greens	MM	Mostly Muffins
CT	Cooking For Two	CHC	Chinese Cooking	SP	Soups
SC	Slow Cooker Recipes	PK	The Pork Book	SU	Simple Suppers
SF	Stir-Fry	RL	Recipes For Leftovers		*NEW* February 1/07
MAM	Make-Ahead Meals	EB	The Egg Book		

Cookbook Author Biography

CODE	CA$15.99 Canada US$12.99 USA & International
JP	Jean Paré: An Appetite for Life

Most Loved Recipe Collection

CODE	CA$23.99 Canada US$19.99 USA & International
MLA	Most Loved Appetizers
MLMC	Most Loved Main Courses
MLT	Most Loved Treats
MLBQ	Most Loved Barbecuing
MLCO	Most Loved Cookies

CODE	CA$24.99 Canada US$19.99 USA & International
MLSD	Most Loved Salads & Dressings
MLCA	Most Loved Casseroles
MLSF	Most Loved Stir-Fries
	NEW April 1/07

3-in-1 Cookbook Collection

CODE	CA$29.99 Canada US$24.99 USA & International
QEE	Quick & Easy Entertaining
MNT	Meals in No Time

Lifestyle Series

CODE	CA$17.99 Canada US$15.99 USA & International
DC	Diabetic Cooking

CODE	CA$19.99 Canada US$15.99 USA & International
DDI	Diabetic Dinners
LCR	Low-Carb Recipes
HR	Easy Healthy Recipes
HH	Healthy in a Hurry
	NEW March 1/07

Special Occasion Series

CODE	CA$20.99 Canada US$19.99 USA & International
GFK	Gifts from the Kitchen

CODE	CA$24.99 Canada US$19.99 USA & International
BSS	Baking—Simple to Sensational
CGFK	Christmas Gifts from the Kitchen
TR	Timeless Recipes for All Occasions

CODE	CA$27.99 Canada US$22.99 USA & International
CCEL	Christmas Celebrations

Order ONLINE for fast delivery!

Log onto **www.companyscoming.com**, browse through our library of cookbooks, gift sets and newest releases and place your order using our fast and secure online order form.

Buy 2, Get 1 FREE!

Buy any 2 cookbooks—choose a **3rd FREE** of equal or lesser value than the lowest price paid.

Title	Code	Quantity	Price	Total
		$	$	
DON'T FORGET to indicate your FREE BOOK(S). (see exclusive mail order offer above) please print				
TOTAL BOOKS (including FREE)				
TOTAL BOOKS PURCHASED:			$	

	International	USA	Canada
Shipping & Handling First Book (per destination)	$ 11.98 (one book)	$ 6.98 (one book)	$ 5.98 (one book)
Additional Books (include FREE books)	$ ($4.99 each)	$ ($1.99 each)	$ ($1.99 each)
Sub-Total	$	$	$
Canadian residents add GST/HST			$
TOTAL AMOUNT ENCLOSED	$	$	$

Terms

- All orders must be prepaid. Sorry, no CODs.
- Prices are listed in Canadian Funds for Canadian orders, or US funds for US & International orders.
- Prices are subject to change without prior notice.
- Canadian residents must pay GST/HST (no provincial tax required).
- No tax is required for orders outside Canada.
- Satisfaction is guaranteed or return within 30 days for a full refund.
- Make cheque or money order payable to: **Company's Coming Publishing Limited** 2311-96 Street, Edmonton, Alberta Canada T6N 1G3.
- Orders are shipped surface mail. For courier rates, visit our website: **www.companyscoming.com** or contact us: **Tel: 780-450-6223 Fax: 780-450-1857.**

Gift Giving

- Let us help you with your gift giving!
- We will send cookbooks directly to the recipients of your choice if you give us their names and addresses.
- Please specify the titles you wish to send to each person.
- If you would like to include a personal note or card, we will be pleased to enclose it with your gift order.
- Company's Coming Cookbooks make excellent gifts: birthdays, bridal showers, Mother's Day, Father's Day, graduation or any occasion …collect them all!

☐ MasterCard   ☐ VISA   Expiry ___ / ___ MO/YR

Credit Card # _____

Name of cardholder _____

Cardholder signature _____

Shipping Address Send the cookbooks listed above to:

☐ **Please check if this is a Gift Order**

Name: _____

Street: _____

City: _____ Prov./State: _____

Postal Code/Zip: _____ Country: _____

Tel: (___) _____

E-mail address: _____

Your privacy is important to us. We will not share your e-mail address or personal information with any outside party.

☐ **YES! Please add me to your News Bite e-mail newsletter.**

Simple Suppers has your dinner dilemma solved! Have fun mixing and matching from our extensive selection of side, salad and entree recipes. Or follow our suggested combinations for a delicious, nutritionally-balanced meal, every time. It's meal planning made simple!

Company's Coming COOKBOOKS®

Quick
&
Easy
Recipes

Everyday
Ingredients

Canada's
most popular
cookbooks!